Those Who Can

Studies in Criticality

Shirley R. Steinberg
General Editor

Vol. 507

The Counterpoints series is part of the Peter Lang Education list.
Every volume is peer reviewed and meets
the highest quality standards for content and production.

PETER LANG
New York • Bern • Frankfurt • Berlin
Brussels • Vienna • Oxford • Warsaw

Tanya Merriman

Those Who Can

A Handbook for
Social Reconstruction and Teaching

PETER LANG
New York • Bern • Frankfurt • Berlin
Brussels • Vienna • Oxford • Warsaw

Library of Congress Cataloging-in-Publication Data
Names: Merriman, Tanya, author.
Title: Those who can: a handbook for social reconstruction
and teaching / Tanya Merriman.
Description: New York: Peter Lang, 2018.
Series: Counterpoints; v. 507 | ISSN 1058-1634
Includes bibliographical references.
Identifiers: LCCN 2017037211 | ISBN 978-1-4331-4969-6 (hardback: alk. paper) |
ISBN 978-1-4331-2973-5 (pbk.: alk. paper) | ISBN 978-1-4331-4966-5 (ebook pdf) |
ISBN 978-1-4331-4967-2 (epub) | ISBN 978-1-4331-4968-9 (mobi)
Subjects: LCSH: Critical pedagogy. | Culturally relevant pedagogy.
Classification: LCC LC196.M47 | DDC 370.11/5—dc23
LC record available at https://lccn.loc.gov/2017037211
DOI 10.3726/b11845

Bibliographic information published by **Die Deutsche Nationalbibliothek.**
Die Deutsche Nationalbibliothek lists this publication in the "Deutsche
Nationalbibliografie"; detailed bibliographic data are available
on the Internet at http://dnb.d-nb.de/.

Thank you Dr. Shirley Steinberg for making this book possible.
Thank you Dr. Leila Villaverde for thinking this book was possible.
For O.B., J.K., E.B. E.B., btm: Above and beyond.
Thank you B.B., C.S., and T.V.W. (you kept me going.)
This book is for Tia and Teddy, as is everything I do.
And, especially, for Troy, you are the best thing to ever
happen to me. Thank you, always.

TABLE OF CONTENTS

INTRODUCTION

Historically, the role and purpose of public schools has been debated. Are public schools supposed to maintain existing power structures or dismantle them? Critical pedagogy, as a philosophical approach to education, has emerged as a response to this age-old question, posing that the critical element for an educator's practice is that all decisions are inherently political and social. This study traces the development of a critical pedagogy within one educator's personal history, and examines the implications of critical pedagogy from this educator's perspective. The study draws from the educator's years of practice and reflection and reads as a handbook for other educators to use in the implementation of critical pedagogy. Divided into four sections, the first proposes that all teachers share a set of responsibilities, and carries out an assessment of the educator's work using these responsibilities as a benchmark. The second section considers teaching and learning from the perspective of a critical pedagogy. The third section offers possibilities for a critical pedagogy that others may use, including a school design and lesson plans. The last section includes a timeline of significant events in the history of public schools as well as a glossary of terms and a bibliography. This study relies on multiple research methodologies. Essentially an action research project, it incorporates historical inquiry and interpretation of the written contributions that some of the most significant critical education and critical race theorists have given to the world of educational pedagogy. Challenging the current trend of simplified and teacher-proof classrooms, this study concludes that critical pedagogy offers both ways to meaningfully question the work of teaching and ways to find answers.

· 1 ·

TEACHING IN THE FRAY

There is a conflict that exists in American classrooms. This tension has existed historically and exists now. Are schools neutral spaces where information is disseminated and acted upon or the location for the emergence of democracy, liberation, and freedom? Are they the space where the power structures and social hierarchies are produced and preserved? It is this dichotomy posed in 1916 by philosopher and educational reformer John Dewey, who wrote about the hope and possibility for democracy as well as what critical education theorist Michael Apple in the 21st century calls the maintenance of hegemony that is inextricably linked to the current state of American public-school education. From the intent of the material used to prepare students to the unanswered socio-politically driven concepts of citizenship, voice, value systems, and vocation, candidates in teacher preparation programs are projected to grapple with philosophy of education courses that conflict with their teaching experience once they enter a public school. The ideals espoused in philosophy classes seem to be at odds with the experiences of urban public-school teachers. The short answer to these questions is that schools are not neutral places. In her 2001 article, There is no Race in the Schoolyard, Amanda Lewis explains that teachers need to strongly resist the notion that "…schools are seen merely as transmitters of useful knowledge; as neutral instructional sites rather than as cultural and political sites in which prior social order is reproduced" (Lewis, 2001). She goes on to tell us that "Schools are arguably the one of the central institutions involved in the drawing and redrawing of racial lines," and even more significant that "Schools may be one of few places where such racial understandings can be successfully challenged."

Therefore, teachers must simultaneously deliver content in a social context that does not match their preservice philosophical ideals. Teachers are struggling with meaning-making while engaged in the real world of teaching. It is this reality that is addressed by this book. The introduction that follows serves the following two purposes:

- First, to situate the theory itself within the text of this book—a text that attempts to demonstrate how the foundation and implementation of a critical pedagogy takes place; and
- Second, to situate the role of social justice education: critical pedagogy, critical multiculturalism, antiracist education, and social reconstructionism in the history of the American education system. The field of education is dynamic and evolving, so, of course, alternatives have been proposed and even practiced. Still, there is uncertainty in the field as structures and strategies have been introduced at individual schools, systems, and now the nation. The extent to which we organize and classify our pedagogical identities should be directly related to the extent it extends our thinking and supports our work.

Kwame Anthony Appiah reminds us that our social responsibilities extend beyond our immediate orbit: "Our responsibilities are not just to a hundred people with whom we can interact with and see... you cannot retreat to the hundred. You can't simply be partial to some tiny group and live out your moral life there"; this is the truth for educators, especially (p. 88). So, in this spirit we will call the umbrella theory antihate pedagogy. Under this umbrella is the social justice umbrella and under this is the critical theory, critical pedagogy, multiculturalism, culturally relevant teaching, and of course social reconstructionism.

The term "hate crime" is a traditional offense like murder, arson, or vandalism with an added element of bias. For the purposes of collecting statistics, the FBI has defined a hate crime as a "criminal offense against a person or property motivated in whole or in part by an offender's bias against a race, religion, disability, sexual orientation, ethnicity, gender, or gender identity."

Hate itself is not a crime—and the FBI is mindful of protecting freedom of speech and other civil liberties.

So for our purposes, anti-hate education will describe education, teaching, and content that is specifically meant to actively combat bias and the actions that are bias driven. The operative term here is bias. Antihate education acknowledges and actively seeks work against bias and hate in any way that it manifests in our schools.

Similarly, social justice is both concerned content and approach. It is defined by Lee Ann Bell as both a process and a goal. She writes "the goal of social justice education is full and equal participation of all groups in a society that is mutually shaped to meet their needs." As social justice educators we are concerned with providing academically rigorous and excellent classrooms and learning experiences, but we are also concerned with making space for them to question, challenge, and contribute to what and how that rigor is defined. As social justice educators we want our students to be prepared and excited to go on to higher education after their primary schooling, but more importantly, we want them to construct and contribute to a world where anyone that works a full work week is guaranteed food, shelter, access to medical care, and the resources to survive and thrive and care for their families.

Agency and responsibility are central to social justice education; exceptional learning experiences matter for their own sake (and, indeed, providing exceptional learning experiences for underrepresented children is in and of itself a radical act) but also to be transformed into tools for creating social change, justice, and transformation.

Concurrently, to teach from a social justice orientation means we must examine and question justice for whom? Justice from what? Implied in this phrase is that there is injustice.

The broadest term to usefully answer this question is the term oppression. Beneath this umbrella we'll find internalized and personal bias. Institutional and systemic oppression or, what we know conversationally as the isms and the phobias: racism, classism, sexism, ableism, homophobia, Islamophobia. Everyone can and should be compelled to want social justice, but what this looks like in your school may differ depending on the communities you serve and represent. Doing the work of figuring out where we stand on all sides of this equation is necessary and ongoing.

From here we move next to the critical terms: critical theory, critical race theory, critical pedagogy, and critical multiculturalism.

The term "critical" has multiple singular, yet overlapping meanings that apply to our work. We know critical to mean disapproving (she was critical of the movie they chose) and we know critical to mean a certain kind of recognition (the movie received critical acclaim). For educators, critical more often is associated with critical thinking: disciplined thinking that is clear, rational, open-minded, and informed by evidence. So, understandably, critical theory concerns itself with the critique of society, culture, and the humanities. Established originally in Germany at the Frankfurt School in the 1930s, critical theory as a wider discipline asks how society, culture, politics, and ideology are woven together.

Critical educational theory is the examination of how political and ideological systems intersect with our schools. Critical pedagogy is, like all of these terms, complex and will receive more appropriate attention further in this book, but for the purposes of our overview, critical pedagogy is teaching that enacts and reflects these qualities. If Critical Theory is the examination of the underlying questions and concepts, Critical Pedagogy is the practice of working through these questions. Joe Kincheloe and Shirley Steinberg (1997) tell us that critical classroom teachers "informed by a concern with power seek a system of meaning which grants a new angle, a unique insight into the social consequences of different ways of knowing, different forms of knowledge, and different approaches to knowledge production and teaching." (p. 238) Being a critical pedagogue, a critical teacher, means to find new things to know, new ways to teach them, and new ways to learn.

Multiculturalism is loosely understood or even misunderstood in rough, clichéd strokes as tolerance including everyone: the melting pot. Responsible, critical multiculturalism should also seek to include everyone, but in ways that are particular and responsive to that community. Critical multiculturalism is concerned not only with the recognition and tolerance of difference, but with the promotion of equity and the alleviation of subjugation, especially for underrepresented groups.

While social reconstructionism encompasses the qualities of each of these systems, what Social Reconstruction offers, explicitly, that the other approaches do not is that schools are, by design, where the belief systems and behaviors necessary to inequality are created, maintained, and replicated, and schools are also the place where we can undo these forces. This conversation was advanced by W.E.B. Dubois who asserted that "education was useless if it did not foster change", and even more inspiring, that "black people must use education not simply to study the world, but to change it." More than any of these approaches, SRC takes the war against inequality and puts the teachers firmly on the front lines. This is important because it elevates the work of the teacher, or rather, recognizes and affirms the incredible work that teachers do in their classrooms every day. It attests to the extraordinary contributions of those who can: those who teach.

References

Apple, M. W. (1990). *Ideology and curriculum.* New York, NY: Routledge.

> This text is dense and succinct. Outlining the hegemonic, ideological, and systematic nature of power and resources, it draws a very short and straight line between these forces and our classrooms. Have your post-it notes and highlighters ready; you will find that every passage in this book confirms your sense of things and answers your questions. This is one of many books that new teachers must read before they begin their journey.

> Michael Apple writes and lectures about power and education. He is one of the most important critical theorists we have. He is a friend to teachers and students. While his work takes on the intense and difficult nature of how power, politics, race, and class impact our classrooms, it always manages to be hopeful and empowering.

Dewey, J. (1959). My pedagogic creed. In M. E. Dworkin (Ed.), *Dewey on education: Selections.* New York, NY: Teachers College Press. (77–80)

> John Dewey is probably the most read and recognized educational theorist. His focus on development, the role of doing, and child-centered, holistic education has tremendously influenced what we learn about education. Every teacher should do the work to contextualize their theories within the greater realm of critical educational theory.

Kincheloe, J. L., & Steinberg, S. R. (1997). *Changing multiculturalism: Changing education.* Philadelphia, PA: Open University Press.

Lewis, A. E. (2001). There is no "race" in the schoolyard: Color-blind ideology in an (almost) all-White school. *American Educational Research Journal, 38*(4), 781–811.

· 2 ·

HOW TO USE THIS BOOK: YOU DON'T HAVE TO READ THE WHOLE THING, BUT PLEASE READ THIS

The urge to create develops a spark into the idea, followed by the concept and consequent phases of development of the work, creating a constant process of shaping, reshaping, and breaking down and rebuilding. All the while during this process, deep connection with the soul silently informs and steers the rigorous dialogue with mind and the hand.

(Eelco Buitenhuis, 2015)

This book was born of a specific need, first of my own and then on my students, to answer urgent questions in a speedy, but upright manner. It has taken many different forms, each folding in to the next version following new experiences (new schools, new cities, new children). While I wouldn't want to take as much time writing another book, I am ultimately glad that I have been able to concentrate more than a decade's worth of learning into one place for the benefit of my students and other teachers. For the past six years I have been teaching preservice teachers in classes that are designed to explore these issues and situate new teachers within the social, cultural, and political context that they will eventually be teaching within. Having taught nearly one thousand students in this time, I have been able to field many concerns. Most common is, What does this look like in the classroom? Most teachers, recognizing the urgency of this social context, want ready answers, prescriptions, and probably roll their eyes at me when I earnestly explain to them that it is a process; that my answers won't be their answers and that most of the answers can only come once you are physically in the classroom and staring into the faces of your own students. In this time, most of the students have enthusiastically risen to this challenge and, even with the few who have been resistant or incredulous, I have taken their concerns to heart. I have learned from each of them. This book is the result of a perpetual breaking down and reshaping.

Within this request I recognize the concern that some of my students won't be going on to complete additional graduate programs and conduct enough of their own pointed research to fill a book. The reality is that they will be busy. Very busy. So this book is an attempt to solve this problem. My goal is to make some of the stuff a little bit more accessible so that they have a few more of the tools they need to do this urgent work. While the heart and substance are still here, they are just all here in the same place. My only request is that this is a starting place and that you honor your curiosity by following up on the ideas that really grab you.

So, then a couple of messages.

First—No one expects you to read this book page after page, cover to cover. But try to sit through this section. This book can be linear: read from start to finish, but it doesn't have to be. If one section has more immediate importance to you than another, then start there. My suspicion is that very few of us read anything from start to finish anyway. So, instead this book is very much meant to be treated as a handbook. The glossary is very much meant to cognitively support the text in that having a handy definition of a complex concept can make reading about it in context that much more meaningful. I am intentionally using healthy block quotes in some places so you see both how the source supports my thinking, and also conveniently get a stronger sense of the source at the same time. I encourage you to even start at the bibliography and if a particular article resonates with you then put it on your list. Chances are, there is a lot more where that came from.

This book is a user's guide. Which brings me to my second message: This book is in no way meant to be an exhaustive and complete treatment of critical pedagogy and social justice education. It isn't. It isn't even meant to share definitive examples of any aspect of practice. Rather, it is meant to share possibilities for practice. There are a few key areas of practice that I have decided not to address in the book and instead to bring to life on the website. The website offers the space to evolve, update, and expand upon the possibilities, possibly with less formality but definitely with more urgency. The most pressing areas that I have opted not to address at length here are standardized testing,

the intersection of schooling and religion, special education, LBGTQ pedagogy, as well as TESOL, ESL, and STEM subjects. The decision not to address
these issues in depth here is in no way indicative of how important they are.
Instead, they reflect my own experiences and the concepts I am just more
familiar with. On that note, I am an African-American, biracial woman. I am
a black wife and mother: unabashedly preoccupied with the well-being of my
black husband and children. I have mostly taught young African-American
children, but a very diverse array of graduate students. This is just me and it
makes sense to work from where I'm at. However, I will ask that as much as
possible, you do the work of universalizing the concepts and skills to best serve
whoever you and your people happen to be.

Due to the fluctuating nature of both of these discussions I have made the
decision to address them using a different media. There is a website that has
inevitably evolved from the nature and limitations of this book. The website
will hopefully do the job of filling in some of those spaces and establishing the
ongoing process of learning, reflection, and teaching.

How this book works: My version of hypertext

Visiting the local library was one of the most important and enforced
activities of my childhood. On one of these visits, I found a well-worn copy of
an annotated *Alice in Wonderland*. On the cover, within the larger dark pink
and smaller light pink frames, was a black and white etching of tiny Alice in
the forest, about to fight with a gigantic, flying dragon. Her weapon of choice:
the sword.

Inside the book, the world of Alice and her looking glass became dimen-
sional and real for me. Not only were there illustrations that were representa-
tive enough to give shape to some of our favorite images from the story—the
Queen of Hearts and her militia of cards, the Mad Hatter in his misfortune—
yet subtle enough to leave room for the reader's imaginings of the characters and places, the book also had poems tucked in the text; they read back-
ward and forward, up and down. And on each page at the bottom was a little
number that matched a number next to certain words on the page. Next to
the numbers at the bottom of the page were explanations, little stories about
the words or situations that, while being nonessential to the story of Alice
itself, allowed for all sorts of connections and discoveries that I could make
between the story and the outside world.

To me this book was a grown-up book but still allowed for all of the adventure and discovery that reading children's stories did. I didn't need to know
that in chapter II of *Through the Looking Glass*, when the flowers announce the

coming of the Red Queen, Carroll was making a reference to Tennyson's Maud, or that he changed the name of the passion flower to a tiger lily because the passion flower's markings came to associate it with the passion of Christ. But these notes left me with questions: Why did he change the name? Why did the scene of the flowers waiting for the queen remind him of the poem by Tennyson? These notes left me with a feeling of wonder and magic for how much was really happening in this story of Alice's adventures. And I would later understand, they also left me with a sense of ownership and connection to Tennyson and all of the other references that Carroll made. I had a context in which to put these writers and this history—and so I wasn't afraid of them when I would later encounter them in my own adventures; they felt like old friends.

This book engaged me. Later I would also come to understand the performative and web-like quality of the annotated version of Alice, in that opening this book was just like falling down a rabbit hole. I became an Alice; the footnotes often led me to do additional research and make countless connections that were all my own. I chose, like Alice did, to grow small and grow tall. I credit this book for turning me into a life-long Alice. To this day, I make discoveries and connections in that book that, because of new experiences and new things that I have learned, I wouldn't have made 20 years ago.

The evolution of the Internet has turned over a new way of reading and of collecting information. On the Internet, text does not proceed. Any Web page will have visual information, sound, or more written information connected by links embedded within its paragraphs. The concept of text within the context of the Internet is called hypertext. This different way of processing information is called web-based thinking: Different than linear thinking.

This term was first coined by Theodore H. Nelson in the 1960s and, as George Landow (1992) explains, means not only electronic text, a new information technology, and a new mode of publication, but "non-sequential writing—text that branches and allows choices to the reader, best read at an interactive screen" (p. 1).

Landow goes on to explain that hypertext changes the role of the author and the role of the reader as well:

> ...hypertext reconfigures—re-writes—the author in several obvious ways. First of all, the figure of the hypertext author approaches, even if it does not entirely merge with that of the reader; the functions of reader and writer become more deeply entwined than ever. This transformation and near merging of roles is but the latest stage the convergence of what had once been two very different activities...Hypertext,... creates an active, even intrusive reader. (1992, p. 1)

In hypertext, the reader operates much like Alice in the Rabbit Hole: There is no one direction in which to proceed toward his or her goal. In fact, the act of "surfing the Web" may take the voyager in many different directions; this trip does not arrive at any predetermined, convergent point. In the process of surfing—is it on the Web or through a book with annotations—one may end up at any number of places. The reader has control, becomes the authority, and charts his or her own course.

This process calls to mind the relationship between teacher as student and student as teacher, which Paulo Freire (2000) describes in his problem-posing method of education and which has, I believe, tremendous implications for us as teachers and how we, as a whole, perceive knowledge. If the fundamental relationship between writer and reader can be interrupted and the consequential location of power can be shifted, this means the writers of history, the writers of how we see ourselves, can, too, be decentered or reimagined, and history itself can be changed. This grants the readers of history a new type of power—and this leads to a new narrative and a retelling of the old. Ironically, Alice is awakened from her dream when the Red Queen is dwindled down to the size of a doll and Alice picks her up and shakes her.

A powerful and useful description of Internet-based thinking comes from, appropriately enough, an essay on the impact of a networked government, "Homeland Security," by W. David Stephenson. In this essay, Stephenson (2002) describes the limitations created by old technology and the old ways of thinking that were generated from this technology. He contrasts two kinds of thinking. One he associates with older communications media, which he likens to the railroad with its qualities of power and linearity; the second he describes through the analogy of the spider web, reconstructed daily to fit current circumstances, and which he finds reflected in the new communications technology of the World Wide Web. The second system he finds superior in dealing with the current challenges in homeland security because it allows for rapid adaptation to changing conditions. Stephenson goes on to describe the creation of "Internet thinking," originally conceived in 1945 by Presidential Science Advisor Vannevar Bush as the "memex," a device that would mimic the mind's way of working, "organizing information not in a linear fashion but by association" and allowing tremendously greater freedom for users to annotate and connect ideas (2002). Stephenson describes how Ted Nelson, 20 years later, named this concept hypertext to refer to nonsequential, interconnected writing. Stephenson concludes:

> With hypertext...we can now go beyond linear thinking. Instead, we can link a wide range of ideas and thoughts that leave the power in the hands of the reader to explore related topics rather than just a single linear argument. However, allowing us to link various thoughts in a nonlinear fashion is one thing. Capitalizing on it is another. (p. 124)

Breaking with the traditional, linear structure of a text such as this is one way that I hope to capitalize on nonlinear thinking. I thought about my own reading, thinking, and learning habits—what worked best for me. What did I get the most out of? It was texts such as Alice that encouraged my inquiry and my curiosity, texts that allowed me to jump in from my own personal point of departure and then took me beyond this point.

I want to create the handbook that I wanted five years ago when I started teaching. I want this manuscript to be—as we say in our classrooms—"ready for Monday." So that readers can chart their own journey through the worlds of critical theory and social justice teaching, the text will not necessarily be linear or circular, but more web-like instead. This way, readers can choose their own adventures. If there is a question about why a particular thinker refers to another thinker, the reader simply has to turn pages to find information about either one.

In Is There a Queer Pedagogy?, Deborah P. Britzman (1998) writes about reading practices. Quoting Shoshanna Felman (1998), she shows us that:

> to read is automatically to make a dialogic relation with self and text. The reader, then, is obligated to ask, "What is it that I am responding to?" The text and the self-perform differential replies, perhaps in the form of a question, perhaps an argument, perhaps a refusal. In acknowledging this relation—reading as provoking dialogue—reading practices begin with a supposition of difference, division and negotiation. (p. 225)

The heart of critical theory is to question what we know as conventional ways of thinking and being. The text will allow the reader to practice this method of questioning. As readers question the text, the text can question back. The readers can construct a dialogue between the two thinkers, filling in the spaces and the gaps for themselves.

Britzman also explains that how one reads matters. Again, quoting Felman (1998), she discusses the role of reading in the relationship of theory to practice:

There is a constitutive belatedness of the theory over practice, the theory always trying to catch up with what it was the practice, or the reading was really doing. Such belatedness, where the recognition of how one reads drags behind the investment of the immediacy of gathering meanings or getting meaning straight, might allow the reader to theorize the limits of her practices, or what she or he cannot bear to know. (p. 225)

I hope to close the gap a little so that the teacher can be prepared and act in the immediacy of the moment. Having theoretical concepts at his or her fingertips will, I hope, save the teacher some time to focus on the more important work: reconstructing the world. This doesn't mean that the depth of theory or complexity of our application is missing, instead I just want to make the machinery of informed practice a little bit easier to operate.

In *Derrida for Beginners*, Jim Powell (1997) helps us to understand why centers are problematic: The problem with centers for Derrida is that they attempt to exclude. In doing so they ignore, repress, or marginalize others (which become the Other) (Powell, 1997, p. 23).

If the practice of critical pedagogy concerns itself with the ending of the marginalization of the Other, then I hope for this text to be performative. It will decenter the reader within the text, hopefully encouraging the decentering of the reader within his or her own practice.

In the chapter called "Human Science" the idea of the pathic is noted and the invitational character of the world explained. "For example, cool water invites us to drink, the sandy beach invites the child to play, an easy chair invites our tired body to sink in it, etc." (chap. 1, "Human Science," from Researching Lived Experience Massimiliano Tarozzi xx). I hope to create a pathic text: one that invites readers to explore the possibilities of their own work. My goal is for this book to act as a reminder and an assistant to fill that space between theory and practice. It should serve two purposes. The first is making information available to teachers in a way that is accessible and useful. The second is introducing the concepts in such a way that the reader will be inspired and encouraged to continue to explore these worlds on his or her own.

I encourage the reader to read this book as hypertext, as you would if you were doing research on the internet, and probably as you do your planning anyway. Zigzag through it as you see fit. My thinking is that if you come to it looking for information about bell hooks, you will read the biography and then flip to the chapter on responsibilities to see what hooks has to say about theory. From there the path could lead to the glossary to see exactly what is meant by a particular concept, such as the banking system, and then from there to the biography of Freire, and so on, and so on.

Furthermore, if, in my limited design, I didn't provide enough information about a subject, I really, really hope the reader will go to the Internet or to his or her resources to do even more research. This text is in no way an exhaustive explanation of anything; instead, at best, it will set a foundation and spark even more curiosity. I wish the reader all of the fun and adventure I have had so far on my journey.

References

Britzman, D. P. (1998). Is there a queer pedagogy? Or, stop reading straight. In W. F. Pinar (Ed.), *Curriculum: Toward new identities* (pp. 211–231). New York, NY: Garland Publishing. (Originally published in 1995 in *Educational Theory, 45*(2), 151–165).

Buitenhuis, E. (2015). *Bullying in the context of politics, pedagogy and power.* Retrieved May 1, 2017 from http://theses.ucalgary.ca/bitstream/11023/2428/4/ucalgary_2015_buitenhuis_eelco.pdf pg.54

Carroll, L. (2013). *Alice's adventures in wonderland.* New York, NY: W.W. Norton.

Freire, P. (2000). *Pedagogy of the oppressed.* New York, NY: Continuum.

Landow, George. Hypertext: The Convergence of Contemporary Critical Theory and Technology. Baltimore: Johns Hopkins UP, 1992.

Powell, J. (1997). *Derrida for beginners.* London: Writers and Readers.

Stephenson, W. D. (2002). *Homeland security requires Internet-based thinking—Not just technology.* Retrieved November 8, 2005 from http://www.homelandsecurity.org/journal/Articles/Stephenson0102.htm

· 3 ·

A BRIEF HISTORY OF
THE PUBLIC SCHOOL

In the one-room schoolhouse sat students of all ages and abilities. The sole teacher was usually an unmarried woman; sometimes the students were older than the teacher. Using only the most basic resources—slate, chalk, and a few books—teaching and learning consisted mainly of literacy, penmanship, arithmetic, and "good manners." Recitation, drilling, and oral quizzes at the end of the day were the norm in classrooms across America.

(School: The Story of American Public Education, PBS, 2001, p. 1)

The first American public school was opened in Massachusetts nearly 350 years ago. Now, with significant economic, social, and technological advancements, the broad educational landscape has developed to adjust and advance our society, positioning the exchange of information at its core. Central to this global transfer of knowledge is the role of the teacher.

Looking back to the structure of the classroom in the late 19th and early 20th centuries, teachers taught academic basics to students demonstrating a variety of competency levels in a single classroom. As a new group of candidates enters the field, the mandate to develop curricula that resonate with its students regardless of the institution's resources, administrative structure, and relationship with its key stakeholders—parents and community members—becomes just as much of an insurmountable task as teaching the primary grades simultaneously in one room with limited resources.

When one considers the vast and ambitious enterprise of the American public-school system, it could easily seem impossible to come to any specific conclusion as to what it would actually take to bring every child forward. At the onset of the No Child Left Behind Act of 2001, standards-based educational reform inadvertently provides opportunities for students who are low performing, culturally and cognately diverse, advanced level, and/or nonnative English speakers to slip through the cracks. While several advancements have been made in the form of improved test scores nationwide, the return to repetitive drills and quizzes demonstrates that the curriculum gap between the one-room schoolhouse and the public school of today isn't as wide as expected.

The urge to simplify and contain schools in order to provide successful and efficient education opportunities seems logical, considering the range of needs and advantages each individual brings to the equation. Consequently, questions and tensions arise simultaneously when identifying key decision-makers to manage institutional efficiency and reform. As a result of these problems and essential questions, many new teachers begin to contemplate their roles that are guided by the theoretical-based education received in preparation for certification and, ultimately, their work in classrooms.

This conflict leaves these candidates with pressing questions: What is the purpose of schools? Why are the schools that I am entering failing? How long am I going to be able to continue teaching when things seem so difficult? Developing teachers often find themselves reperceiving their views on education. They find that the school and curriculum that they inherited conflict with the needs of the students. Unquestioned faith in problematic ways of thinking about our work, problems like color blindness, the myth of meritocracy or deficit model approaches to teaching can result in students being blamed for the failure of schools to appropriately serve them. When this happens, it is usually the students and teachers who end up suffering and taking the blame, interchangeably.

By looking at the roles of the students, their parents, schools, and administration, teachers can investigate these belief systems and frameworks by asking the following essential questions of each group:

- Students: Are they passive consumers of a mismatched curriculum?
- Parents: How do they best advocate for students when it is not their professional training to do so?

- Schools: What should the preparation programs be doing differently and better?
- Principal and other administrative personnel: How do school leaders balance the range of needs presented by the other invested parties?

These questions suggest the need to reassess the relationship between critical theory/social reconstructivism and practical application in order to understand teaching critical pedagogy, and social reconstructionism and practice are discussed and engaged in the classroom setting, providing ways for meaning-making in urban public schools. These ideas are in contrast to the current efforts to redefine language and educational concepts in schools that have taken on many forms, ranging from curriculum maps and in-service programs to other forms of didactic information employing technology. Despite these efforts, new teachers are still defining themselves as being situated in the fray—embarking in an environment without the historically comprehensive and content-accessible tools to create impact. Consequently, the framework in which these teachers begin their work is a source of intimidation and bewilderment. These new teachers are, as bell hooks (1994) says in her book *Teaching to Transgress*, ready to "allow [their] pedagogy to be radically changed by [their] recognition of a multicultural world, [and] give students the education they desire and deserve" (p. 44). Yet they find themselves working in an environment that seems to completely contradict this effort.

This book presents the context in which today's decision-makers function—whether they are administrators or teachers or educators that teach teachers—and interprets the situation in terms of different positions that educators can take within the divergence. This book, a handbook to SRC, proposes that SRC helps us first understand the context, how these issues came to be, and second, understand the solutions. It explicitly outlines what teachers are required to learn, how to educate in a changing educational landscape, and strategies for responding to the needs of students at various levels. Presenting the terminology as core elements of curriculum management, this manual provides easily identifiable applications that enable teacher candidates to gain a comprehensive understanding of critical theory and pedagogy.

Originating in the Frankfurt School, a group of German philosophers and social theorists who were heavily influenced by Marx, critical theory is chiefly concerned with the dynamics of freedom and oppression, and with explaining and undoing these conditions.

They have emerged in connection with the many social movements that identify varied dimensions of the domination of human beings in modern societies. In both the broad and the narrow senses, however, a critical theory provides the descriptive and normative bases for social inquiry aimed at decreasing domination and increasing freedom in all their forms (Bohman, 2005).

The work of Paulo Freire, a Brazilian educator, is significant and must be mentioned in order to present a historical overview of critical pedagogy. It is of primary importance to educators because his work focuses on education systems and classrooms. From his work, a critical pedagogy emerges that is a practice of teaching that serves the basic goal of critical theory: emancipation of the oppressed.

Viewing this work as a life-changing text, many new teacher candidates accept these theories of dual learners and educators and latch on to these ideas, but once they emerge from the graduate-school classroom and enter the secondary-education arena, they are not able to/do not have the language to translate from a theoretical framework to a practical one.

If Critical Pedagogy is the older brother in the Social Justice Family in education then Social Reconstructionism is the younger, but cooler sister. Perhaps less popular in the larger discussion, while the largest challenge to applying a Social Justice Pedagogy is convincing people that it belongs in schools in the first place, SRC directly addresses the connection between schools and social change.

According to J. Zacko Smith,

> As an educational philosophy, educational institutions at all levels are viewed as the main means by which students are prepared to reconstruct the systems through which inequality and the oppression and marginalization of other people occur. Educational reconstruction purposefully and explicitly requires that our schools function as change agents, empowering students to question the very systems in which they live and work, and to create a society that is more equitable and just. (2013, p. 1)

Social Reconstructionism gives us a vocabulary for upholding and legitimizing our work. With SRC we have the words and ideas we need to convince those who doubt that this is exactly what we should be doing in our schools. When we are confronted with the notions that schools should operate like businesses, with hard numbers and test data determining our effectiveness, or worse that conversations about race and injustice do not belong in schools, Social Reconstructionism tells us otherwise.

Emerging as a response to conservative social and educational ideology of the early 20th century and the dismal social economic conditions after the great depression, SRC attempted to react and solve problems with schools as the starting point. Among the major contributors were George Counts, Theodore Brameld, and Harold Rugg. But it was W.E.B. Du Bois who made clearer connections between schools and the connection to the emancipation of newly freed black people. He called for a new school system, led by highly trained black teachers who could "raise them out of the defilement of the places where slavery had wallowed them" (p. 73).

For me, this intentional and purposeful connection is essential. It is a missive. It gives a shape and license to unapologetically make sure that everything I do, all of my content, and all of my approach has the goal of working with my students to question, to act, to see injustice and inequity, and, most importantly, to be empowered to affect change in their own worlds. It deputizes us, as teachers to stand at the front of this change.

Challenges to Applying Social Justice Education

Not surprisingly, there are challenges to critical theory/pedagogy that should be addressed within this introduction. Briefly, these are some of the concerns that arise within the dialogue around this practice:

- Critical theory can be self-contradicting because it claims to encourage freedom of thinking and action but actually imposes a system of thought itself.
- Critical theory is abstract; it lives in the world of academia instead of where it matters. Indeed, it is easy to understand how a theory lives and thrives in universities and colleges that seem to have very little connection to the world the theory is supposed to sustain. As Cornell West (1999) tells us in the essay entitled "The Dilemma of the Black Intellectual," "[i]n good American fashion, the Black Community lauds those black intellectuals who excel as political activists and cultural artists; the life of the mind is viewed as neither possessing intrinsic virtues nor harboring emancipatory possibilities—solely short-term political gain and social status" (p. 305).
- Critical theory has a sexist/European-centered history that must be considered. As bell hooks describes in a conversation with herself about the work of Paulo Freire: "There has never been a moment when

reading Freire that I have not remained aware of not only the sexism of the language, but the way he constructs a phallocentric paradigm of liberation—wherein freedom are one in the same" (p. 48). The same is true of the writing of Du Bois and the other leaders as well. This leaves us with the challenge of contending with this problem and then universalizing the theory as well.

- Resistance. Your educational community may be uncomfortable discussing inequity in the teaching environment. Worse, they may believe it is wrong and that the issues of social injustice have nothing to do with teaching. They may feel unprepared, overwhelmed, and either struggle or shrug. Many teachers may subscribe to what they believe is a colorblind approach and say things like "I don't see race," or "inside everyone is the same." This seemingly well-meaning approach, an approach that many of us were raised with, is flawed and, worse, creates a culture of silencing, devaluing, and missed opportunity.

- If you are in a school that serves primarily white or privileged children, your teaching community may believe there is no need for any social justice educational pedagogy. This thinking is deeply flawed, and in fact, if our goal is large social change, this is exactly who needs this pedagogy the most.

- The math and science teachers may fail to see their role in applying an SRC pedagogy, and insist this is not practical, or even possible for their classes.

- We may feel reluctant to instigate a larger discussion for several reasons: We don't want to make our lives any more difficult and we don't feel competent enough to assume a leadership role when it comes to social justice in our own schools. We don't want to alienate our colleagues or isolate ourselves. If we are already struggling against a lack of support, we may want to retreat to our own classrooms and just shut the door and teach. You may feel unsure of how to start a conversation about race with your colleagues and students of color.

This book is an attempt to challenge and address some of these issues and to demonstrate that despite the issues, critical theory/pedagogy and social reconstructivism are more relevant than imaginable. Moreover, this book is an attempt to bridge the space between the theory and the practice. What has emerged is a theme—the development of one educator's perspective. This work attempts to demonstrate how critical pedagogy and SRC have "been" in my life as an educator. In the following chapters, I will demonstrate how, within my own practice as an educator, I have woven theory into experience, bridged pedagogy and practice, and answered some of these questions for myself. I will also put myself out there, look intrepidly at my own mistakes, and will be honest. It is my hope that by clarifying some of the principles, conflicts, resolutions, and possibilities, my own voice can be added to this long-standing dialogue about schools and the work of being a teacher. No matter what it's called, socially just, reconstructionist, and empowering education is as much about our beliefs, our presence, our approach, and our hearts as it is about our content.

Divided into four sections, this project first examines the role of the teacher. Starting from this point is essential, as educators must first look inward at their own practice and motivations before turning this gaze outward.

The second section explores the tools we have at our disposal to support the work we do. Focusing primarily on building community and practicing reflection, this section focuses on us and how we stay strong.

The third section presents possibilities for a critical pedagogy and SRC in a very practical way. Consisting of a school design and practical approaches, this section offers examples of how the theory can be translated into practice. The last section provides elemental, fundamental information that underlies or is closely related to critical theory. The purpose of this section is to make this information available so that it, too, can assist the application of theory in lived spaces.

References

School: The Story of American Public Education, PBS, 2001.

Bohman, J. (2005). Critical theory. In E. N. Zalta (Ed.), *The Stanford encyclopedia of philosophy*, Winter 2003. Retrieved from http://plato.stanford.edu/entries/criticaltheory/

hooks, b. (1994). *Teaching to transgress*. New York, NY: Routledge.

    bell hooks' writing is often in response to her own experience as a member of the educational system and the academy—both as student and as teacher. She cites Paulo Freire as a mentor because he was the first theorist she read who spoke of the potential for "learning to be liberatory" (hooks, 1994, p. 7). In much the same way, because she believes in the power that learning has to free our students from their individual situations of poverty and oppression, because she speaks to a particular black, female experience, and because she has carved a path as an educator, fearlessly charting her own journey, doing her own work, and because she is endlessly hopeful about education, love, and the human experience, she is an inspiration to any reader.

I can easily recommend her books to anyone, especially teachers, and I often do. Although she is an established member of the academy, her work is especially useful because her language and her approach are real and accessible. Her perspective and advice do not fly over the heads of the people whom they are meant to reach. Instead they come from her real-life experiences, her observations and struggles, and thus they speak to her audience in a way that I believe distinguishes her from every other theorist.

West, C. (1999). *The Cornell West reader*. New York, NY: Basic Civitas Books.

A self-described "non-Marxist socialist" and "Radical Democrat of African Descent," Cornell West is one of the giant scholars of race, class, economics, culture, gender, and social justice today. His work examines everything from classical literature to pop culture to art and music theory to parenting. He is master of both the emotional and intellectual domains. Any time you spend with the work of Cornell West is going to leave you smarter and with a better understanding of your role as an educator and cultural worker.

Zacko Smith, J. (2013). Social reconstruction. Retrieved from http://www.academia.edu/1957998/Social_Reconstruction

· 4 ·

WHY THIS MATTERS NOW
MORE THAN EVER

At the beginning of the 21st century, and for the second time in American history, white births are no longer a majority in the United States. Concurrently, half of American children live in poverty. Schools remain racially segregated and segregated along economic lines as well. Children of color trail their white counterparts on standardized tests, and at the same time the culture of federally mandated, punitive, mandated testing continues to strain moral for teachers, families, and students. We need to struggle to fix this while correctly defining the source of the problems and holding the right people and institutions accountable. We also have to struggle against the pattern of defining our students by their disadvantages. *And*, at the same time, we need to create a space where children from dominant cultural communities can clearly see their place in a hierarchy of privileges and know how to actively dismantle these systems too.

If we take these things into account and align them with our country's history of failing children of color and children with a low socioeconomic background, and with a culture of high-stakes testing, then it makes sense that our schools should have a foundation of preparing students to create social equity. All of our students. We need our students to leave school with the skills to be responsible citizens and contributors to their own democracy. We need our students to be able to actively recognize and respond to injustice. And here is the biggest point about social justice education. It is not a theory that you take down from the shelf on holidays. It is not occasional. This way of teaching, this approach to education is more about our belief in our students, more about our purpose than it is about content and assessment. It is about approach and conviction. It doesn't matter that you memorize the birthdates of the original thinkers; it matters that you see your students as assets and possibilities. It doesn't matter that you know all the terms and win every argument; it matters that you are open to learning, to reflecting, and to growing. And, while I cannot promise a way out of standardized teaching or a way out of being exhausted at the end of every day, I can promise that all of the best teachers and the enduring teachers I know are social justice educators. They see their work, themselves, and their students as a part of a larger purpose and so remain hopeful and optimistic and so they go on to fight another day. This book is for those who can't. Those teachers who can't stop being that 8-year-old who lined up their stuffed animals in their hallways and taught them how to do math. This book is for those teachers who can't wait to see how tall their kids got over the summer break. This book is for those who can't walk through a department store, a thrift store, even the drug store without picking out something for their rooms. And for those who can't give up on their work and their kids and their families. And for those who can't stop fighting, learning and being outstanding are examples of transformation and brilliance in this world.

· 5 ·

COMING FULL CIRCLE—THINKING THROUGH MY OWN EXPERIENCE

In the summer of 1996, I accepted my first official job as an educator at a small elementary school on the South Side of Chicago. I was a tutor in the Chicago Public Schools mandatory summer Bridge Program. I had just completed my degree in English; I was enthusiastic and well intentioned; I was ready to fall completely in love with my students. And I did. They trusted me with secrets about their crushes and best friends. They invited me to come watch them do flips and no-handed somersaults outside at lunch time. They thought their teacher was mean, and so I got to play the "good guy" with no real responsibility or obligation. It was the perfect place to start my work as an educator. Sometime later, this program would be referenced by the president in the State of the Union Address; I thought it was a sign that I was on the right path.

Thankfully, I was only the tutor in that classroom; otherwise the kids would have gotten away with anything and everything. And management was hardly the only place I was unprepared. I couldn't even do long division. Watching some of the students struggling to gain just a few more points on the daily timed reading or seeing twin sisters sob hysterically because one had been promoted to seventh grade and the other would stay behind in sixth was not alone enough to discourage me. But the weariness of the classroom teacher that I worked with and the complete disconnect of the packaged curriculum we were to deliver with the lives of the students, or even my own, was enough for me to realize that becoming a teacher would certainly mean good moments, but I was probably in for some shaky times as well.

Truthfully, this experience left me with a lingering suspicion from my own childhood that to children like me—black, marginalized, poor—schools may actually do more harm than good. My own education, set in a predominantly white, lower-middle-class suburb, was punctuated with episodes of blatant racism and sexism. Perhaps worst was the sometimes overt, sometimes covert fact that the curriculum had very little to do with my life or the lives of children like me.

In fact, from a very early age, I was acutely and painfully aware of what seemed like a deliberate attempt on behalf of the curriculum to antagonize and humiliate children like me. When anything from my culture, much less any culture but the dominant culture, was taught, it was done so in a mocking and demeaning way and left me feeling humiliated. This is what happened when I was visible. It is often difficult to explain to people that being one of the only black children in a predominantly white school setting can be, in itself, a horrible place for a child. While white schools are often considered to be better schools, the price that the "only black child" pays can be enormous. Why, then, was there this same disconnect in a school for black children, with a black teacher, in a neighborhood that prided itself on being progressive and racially diverse?

I learned from a very early age to make myself invisible, to downplay anything and everything about my culture, my family, and my needs that pointed to the fact that I was black. Because I spent my days trying to stay out of the way, my grades quietly suffered, too. But because my mother read to us religiously and our house was overflowing with books, quite by accident, I started to excel in my English classes. I found myself having to make the choice of conforming to the completely Western curriculum because I loved to read and write so much. I wondered if this was the same experience of my students, at least the ones who managed to succeed. What about the students who fell through?

My good English grades got me into college, where I believed another experience was awaiting me. But I quickly found that it wasn't much different at all, except now my professors and fellow students had more sophisticated and seemingly valid ways of keeping me in my place. This was when I began to realize that not only did I look different, but I thought differently, too.

While I became increasingly alienated from my own classroom experience, I became more and more aware of those on the outside who were thinking differently. I decided to pursue my master's degree and at the same time began teaching at a boys' Catholic high school that served a 100% African-American population. While I began my master's degree confident that this urban, progressive institution would point me in the right direction and equip me with the tools I needed to best serve my students, what I found was more of the same. The more I taught and exposed myself to the lives of my own students, the more dismayed I became. Yet despite being encouraged to give up my crusade and "just teach my subject," I remained convicted. I knew that I was meant to function as more than just a contrivance in the lives of my students. At this point I didn't even know that concepts such as positivism or social justice existed. I just knew I was right and that I had my work cut out for me. Not only was the world waiting, but it always seemed that in order to defend my own beliefs I had to know four times as much as everyone else (those that defended the status quo). Thankfully, when I looked at my students, I felt inspired to get the job done.

Something else was shifting in my consciousness, too. A question was forming: If schools were the place where so many children were hurt and told lies about who they were and how the world should be, couldn't schools also be the place where it was made right? And not just for the children who were hurt, but for all children? All children are hurt by the lies that are manufactured within the classroom's four walls. No child by his or her own nature wants a world built on suffering and lies.

Then I found my clue to what I knew must have existed all along. In one of my classes, the professor introduced the ideas of Paulo Freire and William H. Watkins. Her suggestion was simple, really; after introducing Dr. Watkins' "Black Curriculum Orientations: A Preliminary Inquiry," she thought that as teachers of black children we might want to situate ourselves within one or more of the "orientations" so that this would guide our own work. Embedded in his discussion of W. E. B. DuBois and the social-reconstructionism orientation were the words that would completely reroute my journey as a teacher: "Black People must use education not simply to study the world, but to change it" (Watkins, 1993, p. 334).

Then I knew that there were shoulders to stand on, and my transformation from teacher to politically conscious, critical, social-reconstructionist educator began. My new job was to get my hands on as many books and articles like this one as possible. When I continued with my doctoral degree,

I was amazed and relieved to find that there was a tremendous and lively body of work that could inform my teaching and guide my journey. I entered the world of social-justice education and critical theory, and my questions began to change.

Much to my surprise, delight, and relief, I found that there is an entire universe of social-justice education and critical theory to explore and employ. I started to learn the deeper meaning and history of all of these concepts and more. We can choose to call ourselves social-justice educators, critical pedagogues, social reconstructionists, activists—the most important thing is recognizing that as William Ayers and Quinn (2005) tell us in the series forward to See You When You Get There, "rather than a fad or a trend, teaching for social justice can be thought of as the nucleus of the entire educational enterprise" (p. vii). I have many times learned the hard way that if we want to advocate for our students and for critical pedagogy in an educational climate that is invested in protecting the status quo, we must be even more heavily armed than the social injustices that we hope to dismantle. A primary intention of this project is to make this work just a little bit easier.

In the summer of 2006, 10 years after beginning my work as a classroom tutor, I was asked to teach classes on curriculum and critical pedagogy for a graduate program that prepares art teachers to begin their own journeys. During those 10 years, I had collected an abundance of information and ideas, and I had evolved from being an eager, gullible, and unprepared amateur to someone who had something to share and who had lived to tell. Most important, I was ready to come full circle and to begin a brand new journey.

This project is written with an audience of teachers in mind, of course. If we look at current data about who enters (and who leaves) the field of education, this audience, this teacher is probably a young, white woman with the desire to effect real change in her classroom and the genuine intention of connecting with her students. She then may (and should) have questions like the questions my own students have: How can I, as a white woman, meaningfully connect with inner-city kids, or even be taken seriously, for that matter? Or perhaps this teacher is a young woman of color who is coming from a slightly different place in terms of her own identity, but wants to make sure that she has all of the tools she will need to advocate for her own students when she considers that the racial and cultural climate of most schools where "her" children are being educated is possibly hostile and detrimental to them (Michie, 2005). Still, let's say she is a white teacher who plans on teaching in a district that serves a primarily white, middle-class student. She wants to implement a critical multicultural pedagogy, not just for the benefit of the smaller number of children of color, but because she knows that all children will benefit from this curriculum, this pedagogy. This project is written with this teacher in mind as well.

My career as a student/educator often has been haunted by a sense of missed opportunity. Every time I learn something new, I think of 10 situations in which I could have made a difference, I could have better explained something, I could have protected a child, had I only learned about this or that sooner. This project is a handbook, a digest of all of the information, the vocabulary, the theorists, the lessons that I have encountered along the way. The hope is that my audience of teachers will read this and not just scratch the surface, feeling confident that now she "gets it" and can scratch critical pedagogy off her list, but rather, she will read it and use it as a tool to access information and to interact with, so that it strengthens her steps. I have made, and continue to make, my own way; this is a map of my steps, which I hope will provide some guidance and, even more important, create opportunities for some meaningful detours.

Being a revolutionary teacher can sometimes be a lonely place. My hope for this project is to also give teachers that are new to the world of critical pedagogy a sense that they are not alone and that others out there can help to build their foundation. In addition to this, I hope to offer some relief to what Joseph J. Schwab (1978) refers to as the "impossible role of the teacher" (p. 37). This dilemma is that "the teacher must also be the learner," and this can be increasingly difficult considering the many responsibilities the teacher already carries. What I hope to create is a user-friendly handbook of sorts, a field guide to the battle for our children's minds.

References

Ayers, W., & Quinn, T. (2005). Series forward. In G. Mitchie (Ed.), *See you when you get there: Teaching for change in urban schools* (pp. vii–ix). New York, NY: Teachers College Press.

Michie, G. (2005). *See you when we get there: Teaching for change in urban schools.* New York, NY: Teachers College Press.

Schwab, J. J. (1978). Science, curriculum and liberal education. In I. Westurbury & N. J. Wilkof (Eds.), Chicago, IL: University of Chicago Press.

Watkins, W. H. (1993). Black curriculum orientation: A preliminary inquiry. *Harvard Educational Review, 63,* 321–337.

· 6 ·

METHODOLOGY—CONSTRUCTING
MEANING THROUGH MY OWN
EXPERIENCE

Realization of this project has been the result of a playful tension between research and results, questions and answers. I didn't realize seven years ago, when the initial inquiry and writing began, that I would end up teaching a group of teacher candidates myself, and this destination would end up bringing my project full circle. Such is life, of course, and I believe this is another testament to the circular or web-like quality of learning that underlines this entire project.

In order to realize this project, I have become a bricoleur: "a maker of quilts, or one who assembles images into montages" (Denzin & Lincoln, 2000, p. 4).

There are many kinds of bricoleurs—interpretive, narrative, theoretical, political. The interpretive bricoleur produces a bricolage that is a pieced-together set of representations that are fitted to the specifics of a complex situation. "The solution [bricolage] which is the result of the bricoleurs method is an emergent construction" that changes and takes new forms as different tools, methods, and techniques of representation are added to the puzzle (Denzin & Lincoln, 2000, p. 5).

All teachers are bricoleurs, and I believe this process mimics the processes of teaching and learning themselves. So it turns out that this is a wholly appropriate way to approach conducting research that is in service to education and improving education. In doing so, I have employed many methods of research, inquiry, testimonio, interpretation of text, and analysis of practice in order to answer my own questions and construct one completed puzzle.

This is at heart an action-research project. Action research is the "study and enhancement of one's own practice" (May, 1993, p. 224); the study of my own practice was guided by one question: What is the essential information that a candidate would need to begin their practice with a "head start?" How can I offer this information to teachers in a way that is authentic and acknowledges their journey, their way-making? How can I put it together in a way that adds meaning to their journey? How can I create a map, or a field guide, using my own experience as a template? Of course, in keeping with the bricolage, these questions have changed shape as this work developed, and my experience as well as my perception of the necessary routes or tools has changed and built upon themselves.

One of these changes is becoming aware of the tension between theory and practice. My work as an academic leader of teachers is a constant negotiation between the need for and the usefulness of theory and research. The work of primary and high-school teachers resides in the precarious place between "working" and "professional" class, a "pink collar" profession occupied primarily by women, and so therefore easily dismissed as less than professional. Action research plays a role in the political positioning of the education field. Read M. Diket (1997), quoting Sagor, tells us that "as long as teaching remains a profession where isolation is the norm, where the knowledge that informs practice comes from outside the classroom, and where the quality control officers are removed from the classroom, teaching will be more like a blue collar job than an intellectual professional pursuit" (1997, p. 241).

Taking control of the research that is conducted about and delivered to our own profession ultimately changes both external and internal perception of the role of our work. Again quoting Sagor, Diket (p. 241) tells us that "eliminating these destructive features is essential to the health of our profession and the success of our schools. By changing the role of teachers, we can also profoundly change the teaching and learning process in our schools" (1997, p. 241).

This project is also a historical inquiry. In the chapter entitled "Historical Research Methods in Art Education," Mary Ann Stankiewicz (1997) reports: "Sound historical inquiry requires thorough, painstaking compilation of facts, critical reading of both primary and secondary sources, careful note taking, and establishment of chronologies documenting who did what where and when." (p. 57)

Well-written historical accounts also require attention to why development of a narrative interpretation of facts makes them meaningful and explains their significance to readers who are distant from the events recorded (p. 58).

Creation of this map, this field guide, for teachers has been exactly this, capturing the who, what, where, when, and why. Stankiewicz goes on to describe the work of Mary Dana Hicks, who, in 1893, wrote a paper for the International Congress of Art Instruction. She tells us that not only was Hicks putting the past in service of present needs, "but she was creating an overarching interpretive framework...documenting the past was less important to Hicks than finding meaning in them. Hicks focused on the interpretation of the past in an attempt to make past ideas and events meaningful..." (p. 58).

In this same chapter, the writer provides a table that proposes an overview of historical research processes. The last step is to "write a narrative that interprets the facts through a meaningful story that will hold the reader's interest" (Stankiewicz, 1997, p. 59). This is precisely my hope with this project. I am attempting to collect and organize, through the lens of my own experience, a sample of the past research and dialogue that have taken place around critical pedagogy and social-justice education in order to make it meaningful for new teachers and to put these ideas into service of the present needs of both teachers and the students they work with.

References

Diket, M. (1997). Action oriented study as research. In S. LaPierre & E. Zimmerman (Eds.) *Research methods for art education* (pp. 241–244). Reston, VA: National Art Education Association.

Denzin, N. K., & Lincoln, Y. S. (Eds.). (2000). *Handbook of qualitative research*. London & New Delhi: Sage Publications.

May, W. T. (1997). Teachers as researchers. In S. LaPierre & E. Zimmerman (Eds.), *Research methods for art education* (pp. 223–230). Reston, VA: National Art Education Association.

Stankiewicz, M. (1997). Historical research methods in art education. In S. LaPierre & E. Zimmerman (Eds.), *Research methods for art education* (pp. 55–73). Reston, VA: National Art Education Association.

· 7 ·

THE POWER OF THE TEACHER

Those Who Can't?

First of all, the origin of this dim quote is a George Bernard Shaw play called Man and Superman. It is a love story of sorts or a comedy of manners, that isn't about teachers, or schools and doesn't even have a teacher anywhere central to the story. The quote is from the Appendix to the play and is named the Maxims for Revolutionists (B. Shaw, 1903, p. 334). It is "written" by the main character named John Tanner, M.I.R.C, which stands for member of the idle rich class. In the same section he says that "no man fully capable of his own language can learn another" and that "when domestic servants are treated as human beings it is not worthwhile to keep them."

I believe it is safe to say that maybe the self-declared idle rich are not fully qualified to assess the work of teachers. And how this quote, completely out of context and completely absurd, became one of the most common quotes about teachers is a mystery.

This book is a celebration and elevation of our work. We are those who can. I am, above all things, a fierce advocate for and protector of teachers. Becoming a teacher requires completion of rigorous certification programs, more often than not, a Master's Degree, and even after this, it can be challenging for the most qualified teachers to find jobs. Being a teacher, a good teacher, requires a large level of skill, ability, excellence, and grind. Still, our profession is dismissed and questioned at every step. I work with young teachers that log insanely long hours and that fight through incredibly hard days and still, unfathomably, find themselves unable to meet their student loan payments on their salaries. Our teachers deserve better than to ever be portrayed as those who can't. Our profession deserves better than being portrayed as a fun refuge for the otherwise unsuccessful. Most importantly, our students deserve better. Our real-life students deserve qualified, dedicated, outstanding teachers who can count on the support of their communities to do one of the most important and sacred jobs there is. I can't. I can't and won't let my teachers and students be trivialized without shouting loudly that we deserve better.

That this quote, from a story that has nothing to do with teachers, uttered by a man who identifies himself as idle and rich, seems quite metaphorical for the phenomenon of unqualified lawmakers, academics, and administrators making decisions for those that are actually in classrooms doing the work.

Either way, we will do what we always do; what we do best. Repurpose and reinvent this for our own purposes. We are those who can.

References

Shaw, B. (1903). *Man and superman*. Cambridge, MA: The University Press. Bartleby.com, 1999. Retrieved August 7, 2017 from www.bartleby.com/157/

Shaw, R. P. (2000). *The educational theory of Maxine Greene*. Retrieved October 2, 2001 from www.lesley.edu.journals

· 8 ·

TEN RESPONSIBILITIES
FOR THOSE WHO CAN

...education is politics. When a teacher discovers that he or she is a politician too, the teacher has to ask, What kind of politics am I doing in the classroom? That is, in favor of whom am I being a teacher? The teacher works in favor of something and against something. Because of that, he or she will have another great question, How to be consistent in my teaching practice with my political choice?

(Shor & Freire, 1987, p. 46)

This chapter comes from a simple question: Why are we teaching? It is my experience that not many teachers have fully explored this question for themselves. Because teachers have so much impact on the lives of the students they teach, they are responsible for unpacking their motives and beliefs. This chapter examines why we must take this responsibility so seriously.

My own reasons for teaching have evolved and shifted over the years. What has remained the same is the fact that the examination of why has deepened my relationship to my work, my colleagues, and my students.

This chapter is an inquiry into practice—an attempt to ask why questions. "Traditionally, qualitative inquiry has concerned itself with what and how questions. Why questions have been the hallmark of quantitative sociology, which seeks to explain and ostensibly, predict behavior. Qualitative researchers typically approach why questions cautiously. Explanation is tricky business..." (Gubrium & Holstein, 2000, p. 503).

1. Recognize the political nature of teaching.

Teaching is political. Since this reality is the very foundation of critical theory and critical pedagogy, acceptance is not optional and there is no hiding behind the so-called neutrality of subject. Everything taught and learned, all of the space between those two points—between teacher and student, between content and medium, and everything else—is "the political." The political is not a transient mass that appears in the classroom during social science or history lessons. Everything we do in the classroom is born from the political and goes back to the political.

Furthermore, and this is important: Education is political for everyone, not only for teachers with "minority backgrounds" or for teachers with students with "minority backgrounds." Every classroom in this world is a political space.

Recognizing, acknowledging, and accepting the political nature of education can be a truly overwhelming job for any educator. Often it means having to reexamine our own practice and immediate situations and face truths that may be difficult or even impossible to deal with. Yet, it is not hopeless. In fact, it's exciting and promising and full of possibility.

This point of recognition in any educator's career is often at once liberating and excruciating. It is liberating because it quiets the voice inside us that tells us that something is widely wrong. It is painful because we have no choice but to face not only the ways that this hurt us as we came through our own educational course, but also the ways in which we willingly and unwillingly reproduce the same system. Remember, this is a reality that many educators, from all different walks and stages, sometimes mildly and sometimes fiercely resist. It is often extremely difficult to relinquish what is comfortable for us and to become defensive as though we are being directly indicted. It is also a realization that can lead to many different, and yet firmly defended, wrong turns. For some, it can lead to immobilization or worse—realization with such a feeling of paralysis that awareness quickly turns to bitterness and the belief that hate and self-righteous complacence are seen as justified, and refusal to grow as an educator is disguised as resistance.

Still, this can prove to be a temporary space. It is at this point that we also see within ourselves the potential for growth, especially when we realize how much there is to learn. It is one stop on a journey through change and toward transformation that will take you to many different places of understanding and ways of being.

In the third chapter of Teaching to Transgress, entitled "Embracing Change," bell hooks (1994) speaks directly to this pain and discomfort and then how these feelings and experiences can be harnessed to create a "transformation of consciousness and a truly liberatory liberal arts education" (p. 7). She describes her work at Oberlin College, where she and another colleague worked to create a space where the issues of changing curriculum and teaching practices could be discussed, without becoming a space where people would "feel attacked or their reputation as a teacher sullied" (p. 10). She describes:

> Again and again, it was necessary to remind everyone that no education is politically neutral. Emphasizing that while a white male professor in an English department who teaches only work by "great white men" is making a political decision, we had to work consistently against and through the overwhelming will on the part of folks to deny the politics of racism; sexism, heterosexism, and so forth inform what we teach. (p. 23)

Going on to discuss the reactions and resistance of her colleagues, she explains how difficult it was for them to reflect on their own practice:

> We found again and again that almost everyone, especially the old guard, were more disturbed by the overt recognition of the role our political perspectives play in shaping pedagogy than by their passive acceptance of ways of teaching and learning that reflect biases, particularly a white supremacist standpoint. (p. 23)

So yes, this initial stage might be punctuated by your colleagues' indignation and defensiveness, and most likely met with the "it will never work" or "we already tried that and it failed, too" strategy. It is also possible that people (including your students) will question your credibility, or, as Barry Kanpol (1998) puts it, "What right do critical pedagogues have to speak for the oppressed and marginalized, particularly when 'speaking' comes out of a middle class university or teaching position" (p. 3). This question will be especially sensitive if you find it difficult to confront your own privilege, but if you are willing, the potential to learn about ourselves and the lives we touch is endless.

You may find that your students, as hooks (1994) tells us, "bitch endlessly" and are "making complaints like, 'I thought this was supposed to be an English class, why are we talking so much about feminism?'" (p. 24). Or, they might add race or class. They, like all of us, may have a difficult time initially accepting the political character of education and may be especially reluctant to face their own roles within it. This is understandable, considering that these roles and identities tie them most closely to their families and communities. hooks (1994) shares from her own experience as a teacher:

> White students learning to think more critically about questions of race and racism may go home for the Holidays and suddenly see their parents in a different light. They may recognize non-progressive thinking, racism, and so on, and it may hurt them that new ways of knowing may cause estrangement where there was none. (p. 23)

The attempts to transform your classroom into a democratic setting where everyone can contribute might be especially difficult for students whose entire educational experience has been rigid, standardized, and teacher-centered. Speaking to the reluctance of many students to participate in the classroom experience, hooks assures us that this is not "a common approach in what Freire (2000) calls the 'banking system of education' where students are regarded as merely passive consumers" (p. 79). Your initial attempts to transform your classroom may be met with suspicion and resistance. After all, isn't it easier for students to sit and be passive consumers than to actively work and participate in the learning process? Unfortunately, in the short run, it is much easier, despite the devastating results in the long run.

Like anything else your students will learn, it requires a good amount of scaffolding on the teacher's part before the student can master the skill, or, in this case, the deskilling and unlearning. This can be especially difficult when the unlearning is still somewhat tender for the teacher. So what, if anything, is there to be hopeful about? Well, this place of tension and chaos is also the exact location of hope and change. It is in this location that the power to give your students the skills that they will need to see their own way in the world exists. It is here that we can help our students to negotiate power and established roles within the world; to challenge oppression and intolerance while, more important, challenging themselves; and to engage in their own lives without fear.

2. Embrace the equation:

- The world you teach in is a world of inequality;
- This inequality is either replicated or interrupted in schools;
- The teacher is the most important factor in this equation;
- The way the teacher stays on the side of good is by learning more and being critically reflective.

The way we stay on the right side is through research, learning, reflection, and transformed practice. This equation is the heart of social reconstructionism and lives in our classrooms in every nuance from how we spend the moments in the morning before our students arrive to how we bring ourselves home at the end of every night.

The bad news: this may not be what you signed up for and indeed (teacher wars: we shouldn't have to fix politics too) the good news: I have yet to work with a teacher who has backed down from this challenge once it is set before them and, better, as a social justice hero you get superpowers and lots of cool gadgets.

3. Examine your own practice.

Accepting the role of teacher/politician must be naturally followed by a close examination of our own position within the political systems that surround us, both local and global. We must commit to a practice of reflection, of praxis. Our teaching must be continually informed by looking closely, objectively, and acknowledging our own capacity for bias and also growth. Then, this information must be synthesized with the theory, the thinking of the giants whose shoulders we stand upon. This is how we nurture, improve, and complicate our teaching. This practice can and should take whatever form that works best for you—in privacy, in community, online, on paper—it must be yours.

We must also confront and reckon with the ways that our own race, gender, social position, sexual orientation, and privilege inform our ways of engaging the world and our students. Social Reconstructionists practice reflection. NO ONE IS EXEMPT. If you are African-American, this might mean examining the ways that internalized racism has shaped your view of African-American culture and how it is performed on the larger cultural stage. It might mean examining the ways in which we inadvertently and unknowingly help to pass certain messages on to children of all races. If you are male, it might mean an examination of your own behavior and of your own expectations of students. Are there ways in which you duplicate or reproduce certain gender roles within your life and your classroom? If you are white, it might mean looking at your treatment of or expectations of your white students as compared to your nonwhite students.

It is very exciting that we all stand to learn from one another's examination and experience. Oppression functions differently and separately as it unfolds its fingertips and reaches into every pocket of our lives. It's there.

It's not good enough to fight for the empowerment of African-Americans if you are still misogynistic or homophobic. We cannot, as Kwame Appiah and Gates (1996) tells us, retreat to the one hundred. If one of us is oppressed, then we are all oppressed. Fighting for LGBTQ rights may not be your particular ministry, but as many critical theorists will say: You are either working for something or against something. Understanding the functions and effects of sexism can only help in our efforts to undo the function and effects of racism. This is good news; it means that while dedicating ourselves to our own particular struggle, we can use our experiences to help others in theirs. And we can benefit from theirs, too.

This is an ongoing process. Just as no one is exempt, no one is ever fully clear of their own biases. What changes over the course of a lifetime is what we do, what we say, how we act, and the choices we make. What matters is that we step up when the time and battle present themselves. In many cases, individuals have an experience or a series of experiences, a turning point when they witness or experience oppression firsthand, and after this their eyes are opened. It is not uncommon for people to refer to this time as becoming conscious or waking up. For many people, after this point, there is no turning back. How far forward they may go depends on the individual and his or her own particular experience.

Many times it is a teacher or a class that provokes a catalyst to this event for a person. Simply seeing and questioning an advertisement and recognizing the ways in which racism or sexism appear in this medium can be enough to shock someone into a completely different realm of existence. Usually this period of growth is characterized by feelings of relief: Finally having a voice and an outlet for a deep pain that has been building within for a long time can be an incredible feeling of relief. It also can be fraught with fear and guilt: fear of being isolated or helpless in the face of this huge revelation; guilt for the feeling that you have been complicit in this pact for so long. At this point, it is so important to read and connect to the experiences and wisdom of others who have had similar experiences. This period may also be characterized by a feeling of vigilance and a need to convert or evangelize everyone around you so they can see as you do. This feeling is often balanced out, depending on the situation, by a need to shut down or just sit this one out. Some situations may seem so big and so hopeless that you might just want to choose your battles and preserve yourself instead.

In *White Privilege: Unpacking the Invisible Knapsack*, Peggy McIntosh (1998) describes how she first became aware of institutional racism. She says that she "was taught to see racism only in individual acts of meanness, not in invisible systems conferring dominance on my group" (p. 3).

Recognizing the existence of institutional inequality and how we all function within it is an important part of confronting ourselves. Ms. McIntosh tells us:

> My schooling gave me no training in seeing myself as an oppressor, as an unfairly advantaged person, or as a participant in a damaged culture. I was taught to see myself as an individual whose moral state depended on her individual moral will. (1998, p. 1)

Cognizance of institutional inequality helps us to work past the initial fear, doubt, guilt, and resentment that these understandings might bring about and to place them in a larger context. Understanding institutional racism helps us to see that we are a part of a larger system. While this does not negate our own individual responsibility, it appropriates it. It also helps to appropriate our feelings of personal guilt and anger and to place them in a broader context. It is through this work that we become the most powerful as educators. Setting an example for students as educators who are courageous enough to face the most painful parts of our own histories and realities will show them how to do this work for themselves.

4. Get comfortable talking about race, class, sexism, oppression and all of that stuff that no one wants to talk about. If your community never has these conversations then situate and position you to be the designated talker. Build your dialogue toolkit so you can be the deputized leader of these discussions in your school community. If you are fortunate enough to be a part of a community that does have these conversations, then always work to be a part of it and to responsibly advance the discussion that is particular to your teaching and learning universe. Sometimes this means focusing on the thinking and not the feeling part of what is going on. Sometimes it means adding what is needed to elevate the conversation beyond comment section nonsense. Sometimes it means reminding ourselves and everyone else to back up what we are saying with evidence and research. Sometimes it means asking questions; more often it means just listening.

In the article I Don't Want to Hear That (2008), Angelina Castagno describes how "White educators are reluctant to name things that are perceived as uncomfortable or threatening to the established social order. In other words, they possess a strong desire for comfort and ideological safety within their classrooms and the school walls. White educators also tend to hold a shared allegiance to the status quo, presumably because it generally works for us" (Castagno, 2008, p. 315).

Generally, most educators are reluctant to have these conversations in schools because of the risk. There is the risk of offending someone, the risk of escalation, the risk of being distressed, and the risk of getting things wrong. And why wouldn't there be? If you haven't acquired the skills to facilitate these conversations in your own schooling, you are unlikely to have them now as a teacher. I would like to remind us, though, that there is greater risk in not having these conversations. Castagno reminds us that, "teacher silence in the face of student race talk served to support and possibly perpetuates racist beliefs and actions" (Castagno, 2008, p. 322). When these conversations are silenced the denial that comes with color blindness is acerbated by a *colormuteness* (Castagno, 2008, p. 208). This can only lead to confusion, more distress and reinforcing of negative thinking, at the very least. It is our job to acquire and refine these skills. And anyway, the students already have an active exchange concerning race, class, and gender. We would be foolish to think they didn't. It is hugely irresponsible and risky not to engage and evolve their existing schemas.

5. Establish your own purpose for education.

Surprisingly, few teachers have truly established what they believe is the purpose of schooling. Here are some basic questions to consider:

- Why are you teaching?
- What are your students coming to school to receive?
- What are they coming to do?
- What are they being prepared for?
- What do you want for your students?
- What do you want for yourself?

This is an evolving process, and what you want for and from some students may be different from what you want from others. This is an important process because once the purpose of schooling is no longer to assimilate and maintain hegemonic processes, there must be a clearly defined purpose there to fill that space. Reading Bill Watkins (1993), *Curriculum Orientations* was a major catalyst in this process for me because I came to see that my reason for teaching was social reconstruction. Once I was able to identify and name that purpose, it gave shape and definition to my work. It gave me a vocabulary so that I could use language to advocate for my mission and for my students. It gave me something bigger than myself to connect to.

It is important to remember that the world of teaching and learning is, ultimately, bigger than you. Therefore, what you hope your students may get from going to school may be different from what you got from it. I would, ideally, love to see all of my students go to college and graduate school. I want them to become professionals, to establish financial security, and to live healthy, happy lives. Because these goals have been so unqualified for me, it is easy to want to project the same goals on my students—easy, yet this may not necessarily be the best for them. Instead, I think a better goal is that my students have agency to think for and act for themselves no matter what they decide to do when they finish high school. I want them to have choices. I want their vocation, their community, and their family structure to be a result of choices they were able to make, not situations they were forced into. Ultimately, I want them to graduate into shape and contribute to a world where the honest and legitimate work you do, whether that is server, firefighter, nurse, doctor, artist, builder, or teacher like me, equals the ability to take care of yourself and your loved ones, equals access to education and health care, and equals stability and solvency.

My collision with the work of Bill Watkins early in my graduate studies also helped to shape my goals for my students. I want my students to be social reconstructionists as well. I want them to know that they have the ability to study and change the world. Therefore, I must provide opportunities that result in evidence of this ability. I must also make sure they have the skills necessary to change what in the world that they believe needs changing.

6. Embrace theory.

bell hooks (1994) also discusses the importance of theory as "liberatory practice" (p. 59). In Teaching to Transgress, she describes how she came to theory as a child because she was not only questioning the world around her, but also "hurting" from some of the answers. Struggling with her own personal anguish as a child, she saw theory as a means of intervention and a tool for healing. She speaks from a black, feminist perspective, yet she does so in such a way that her voice is universalized. Although she represents a minority, anyone can benefit from her work.

Teaching is perhaps one of the most intellectually and emotionally demanding professions for many reasons. Quite literally, from the time the first bell rings on Monday morning until the last child leaves your room on Friday afternoon, you are on. Planning time is scarce, and often faculty meetings and other structured time end up costing even more. This demand on your time and energy leaves precious little time to read books and apply newfound knowledge to your own practice. What little time you have left over at the end of the day will most likely be devoted to methodology and lesson-plan ideas, not too dense conversations about the larger issues at hand.

There is no denying the incredibly busy nature of teaching; however, even so, I implore you to befriend theorists (like bell hooks) and many, many others. Turning to theory to help realize and work through all of the incredibly difficult challenges we face as educators will save you hours of exhaustion in the end.

Theory also forces us to reorganize and reconstruct our own perspectives. Aristotle tells us: It is the mark of an educated mind to be able to entertain a thought without accepting it. When we engage with theory we are able to entertain these other thoughts and build our empathy, which is crucial to transformative teaching. Considering multiple perspectives is key for our foundation and for our newly forming worldviews as well.

hooks (1994) also recognizes that theory is not "inherently healing"; instead, it is up to us to push theory to this end. She also recognizes that "any theory that cannot be shared in every day conversation cannot be used to educate the public" (p. 67). Theory that is dense and impenetrable obviously will not be useful to you as an educator or a student. Theory should not be some secret code that is transferable only among a select group of chosen members. It should not exclude those that it professes to liberate or inform.

I think one of the most important things any educator can do is invest time in finding the writers that resonate with his or her experiences and struggles. From there, continue to search until a collection is built. As your practice is built, continue to question, challenge, and dialogue with your theorists; continue to share your pain with them.

Lastly, hooks says of theorists: "Their work is liberatory. It not only enables us to remember and recover ourselves, it charges and challenges us to renew our commitment to an active, inclusive...struggle" (p. 74). Continually engaging in a conversation with those who have walked the path before us can restore and mend us as we move forward.

7. Build community.

Tussling with the large and tricky issues of teaching from a critical perspective makes the need for a community of like-minded counterparts a priority. There are several reasons to establish and maintain professional alliances with those who believe in the same truths about education as you do. The first is that, as discussed earlier, doing this work can be isolating. In his study on Teacher Induction, or the mentoring and support of novice teachers in the early years of their careers, Richard M. Ingersoll (2012) found that, "Although elementary and secondary teaching involves intensive interaction with youngsters, the work of teachers is done largely in isolation from colleagues (p. 47). This isolation can be especially difficult for newcomers, who, upon accepting a position in a school, are frequently left to succeed or fail on their own within the confines of their classrooms—often likened to a "lost at sea" or "sink or swim" experience. Don't get lost at sea. Sometime Mohammad must come to the mountain, so if your school doesn't have any kind of formal mentoring program then you need to actively court your mentors and while building those relationships, you should also identify your peers, both locally and virtually, so you can commiserate and build together. If you are the mountain, the master teacher who has some things figured out then reaches out to a teacher that could benefit from your experience and build together.

While I hope that at some point in the near future, all educators will realize the importance of working from a critical perspective, that time has not come yet. Solace can be found in knowing that you aren't alone in this work and that others meet and overcome similar obstacles. The second reason is that you can share information and resources. Most of my colleagues, me included, are usually walking around with several books, articles, Web sites, and various other resources that we share with one another. This is a large part of how we learn from and bond with one another. This is also, not surprisingly, how I learned about the majority of resources that are crucial to my practice. Social media has completely changed what it means to build community, making it possible to connect with other like-minded educators at the click of a button. Social media can be a source of information, feedback, dialogue, and support.

As we build alliances, we are able to fight power with power. In isolation, we have fewer chances of truly effecting change in our classrooms and schools, but together we can pool resources, talent, leadership, and energy. These are hardly the only reasons to establish a community of supportive, like-minded colleagues, but they are some of the most convincing.

If you are teaching in an environment where you are finding it difficult to establish a critical community, reach out beyond your immediate vicinity to others who are connected to organizations that support progressive education.

Attending conferences is a good way to link with people and join forces with individuals who are working toward similar educational goals. Try, when possible, to maintain relationships with classmates who are like-minded and have similar education goals, especially if you were part of a progressive, critical teacher-training program. This is especially important because it is in our own training programs that the foundation is set for working collaboratively and across disciplines. This undertaking is not always as easy as it seems it should be. Lastly, because of the sometimes intense and emotional nature of the work we do and the friendships we may forge out of this work, it is also important to put mechanisms in place to manage the intensity and nurture the ties so that these friendships can continue to be a source of support and validation.

8. Build community with the right people.

As important as it is to build community, it is more important to align yourself with the right people and distance yourself from the wrong people. Schools are often intense, contentious spaces and there is often a need to vent or to complain. This is fine, even healthy at times, but learn to recognize healthy venting and be careful not to vent with those that don't do much of anything else. Be mindful. Give yourself some time to get it out of your system and then move on to more constructive and productive uses of your time and energy. Align yourself with other teachers that support you and bring you up, inspire you to do better, not bring you down. These teachers may not be your own age or look like you, so stretch yourself out of what you are ordinarily comfortable with so you can find the right allies and protect yourself from the unhappy or negative people in your work environment. If there aren't other Social Reconstructionists at your school then reach out. You have at your fingertips the global teacher's lounge. Just clicks away are allies for every possible intention you have. Be aggressive and creative about using social media to network and build community. In fact, even if you have a strong community at your school, you should do this anyway. Creative, productive, purposeful use of social media for networking and building community is a powerful way to expose yourself to others' ideas and practices and this will only strengthen your own practice as well.

9. Learn about happiness.

> What I discovered is that happiness is not something that happens. It is not the result of good fortune or random chance. It is not something that money can buy or power can command. It does not depend on outside events, but, rather, on how we interpret them. Happiness is, in fact, a condition that must be prepared for, cultivated, and

defended privately by each person. People who learn to control the inner experience will be able to determine the quality of their lives, which is as close as any of us can come to being happy. (Csikszentmihalyi, 1990, p. 2)

In his groundbreaking book on the nature of happiness, including the possibility of happiness at work called Flow, Mihaly Csikszentmihalyi tells us that those that find happiness at work are those that see "opportunities for action where others did not, by developing skills, by focusing on the activity at hand, and allowing themselves to be lost in the interaction so that their selves could emerge stronger afterward." Perhaps no other job in the world offers so many possibilities for happiness and so many possibilities for misery; the choice is yours. Figure out what part of teaching you most enjoy, and focus there. Let that be the part of the day that you look forward to. If it is the people that you work with that you need to defend your happiness against, then reread #6 and line up your happiness crew. Make a strong effort to organize your classroom space and procedures so that you are able to focus more on the things you enjoy. If you have questions about how to do certain things or make certain things work, then consult the teachers in your community that have strengths in the areas you want to learn more about and then work it until you figure out what works for you.

Be careful not to confuse what is meant by creating happiness and controlling the inner experience. In no way does this mean that no matter what you force a smile and pretend to be someone or something you are not. It also doesn't mean that you "get over" any serious concerns or infractions that you are dealing with at work, or in life, for that matter. What it does mean is that by building upon, and putting our focus on the things that do bring us joy and happiness, it is possible to have more good days than bad and to set yourself up so you are guarded against burnout and so you can flourish in your career. There is no prescription for this and it may take more than a few tries, but it can be done. Happiness can happen. Seek out the happy teachers in your world and learn from them. We are talking and writing a lot about the millions of ways that teachers are unhappy and discouraged in this profession. But, there are many teachers, at different stages in their careers, in different roles and serving different communities that are thriving. Learn from them and make a similar path for yourself.

10. Give time time. Trust in experience. This might sound a little debatable, but hear me out. There are numerous studies that point to the high rate of teacher turnover and burnout. There are different ways of looking at this

phenomenon, after all, other professions have turnover, and people leave the profession for different reasons. The way that I look at it is that teacher training programs are expensive and in no way is it a good idea to spend or finance thousands of dollars for an education that you'll never even get to really put to use. Even worse than the financial cost is the psychic cost. New teachers are invested, both intellectually and emotionally. This is why teaching is referred to as a calling. I have seen too many teachers, after those challenging first years, leave the profession and never get a chance to master their own practice much less realize their big dreams. The young teachers I've seen are actually fleeing from stressful, chaotic, unsupportive environments that, as Richard M. Ingersoll puts it, cannibalizes its young. Here is what I tell my students before they graduate: It is noble to want to do the hardest work, but there are happy schools in every neighborhood. If you are chewed up within your first two years, this serves no one, least of all your students. Find a happy, functional school with a support system for new teachers, in any neighborhood. Give yourself a chance to get your sea legs, figure out your toolbox, and establish your practice. Once you have done this, if you are serving a community you want to serve then continue and if you want to move to a different, perhaps more underserved community, then you will go to that school stronger, smarter, and more resilient. This is what's best for you and your students. Trust experience and until you have experience, trust in theory.

In the same way, if you are a master teacher, if you have been teaching for a stretch, give yourself permission to explore other areas of education if this is what calls you, especially if you feel tired or that you are in need of a break. Do this proactively so that you don't end up burnt out or worse. Ultimately, we are educators. Thinking of ourselves as educators means we can imagine more possibilities for our practice and escape the flatness of the teaching profession that deters many from ever considering teaching as a career and drives out many of the most talented because they can't see more potential for personal, professional growth. We need to get past the guilt associated with ever wanting to leave the classroom, either temporarily or not, to do more within our schools. This doesn't mean you couldn't stick it out and it doesn't mean you abandoned your kids, either. Justin Baeder (2012) expresses this in his article for the EDWeek Educational Journal, when he writes that "One of the chief challenges to the teaching profession's status as a profession is its flatness. A first-year teacher has the same duties and working conditions as a 30-year veteran, and while the latter may be higher on the pay scale, not much else changes as a teacher (or a principal, for that matter) gains experience and expertise." (p.1) this is only true for the unimaginative social reconstructionist. There are a million ways to serve your students and community as an educator. If exploration of different options is what you need to stay passionate about your work, then this is what's best for everyone.

References

Appiah, K. A., & Gates, H. L., Jr. (Eds.). (1996). *The dictionary of global culture.* Toronto, ON: Vintage.

Baeder, J. (2012). *Unflattening the teaching profession.* Retrieved from August 7, 2017 from http://blogs.edweek.org/edweek/on_performance/2012/04/un-flattening_the_teaching_profession.html

Castagno, A. E. (2008). "I don't want to hear that!": Legitimating whiteness through silence in schools. *Anthropology & Education Quarterly, 39*(3), 314–333.

Csikszentmihalyi, M. (1990). *Flow: The psychology of optimal experience.* New York, NY: Harper & Row.

Gubrium, J. F., & Holstein, J. A. (2000). Analyzing interpretive practice. In N. K. Denzin & Y. S. Lincoln (Eds.), *Handbook of qualitative research* (pp. 487–508). London & New Delhi: Sage Publications.

hooks, b. (1994). *Teaching to transgress.* New York, NY: Routledge.

Ingersoll, R. M. (2012). *Beginning teacher induction: What the data tells us.* Retrieved from http://www.edweek.org/ew/articles/2012/05/16/kappan_ingersoll.h31.html

Kanpol, B. (1998). *Critical pedagogy for beginning teachers: The movement from despair to hope.* Retrieved March 18, 2008 from http://users.monash.edu.au

McIntosh, P. (1998). *White privilege: Unpacking the invisible knapsack.* Retrieved from http://www.utoronto.ca/acc/events/peggy1.htm

Shor, I., & Freire, P. (1987). *A pedagogy for liberation: Dialogues on transforming education.* South Hadley, MA: Bergin & Garvey Publishers.

Watkins, W. H. (1993). Black curriculum orientation: A preliminary inquiry. *Harvard Educational Review, 63,* 321–337.

· 9 ·

REFLECTION

For Paulo Freire (1972) reflective practice is intertwined with theory: "For apart from inquiry, apart from the praxis, individuals cannot be truly human. Knowledge emerges only through invention and re-invention, through the restless, impatient, continuing, hopeful inquiry human beings pursue in the world, with the world, and with each other." Only through this aware struggle can we achieve praxis, or truly transformational teaching practice. John Dewey (1959) maintained that reflective thinking was necessary and urgent for any act of creation, including teaching: "Reflection thus implies that something is believed in (or disbelieved in), not on its own direct account, but through something else which stands as witness, evidence, proof, voucher, warrant; that is, as ground of belief." (p. 120) So, if we build upon the idea of praxis, we have change and reinvention of our teaching that is based on thoughtful, systematic challenging and reconstruction of our own beliefs with evidence and new perspectives.

Many have built from here, suggesting different processes and methods through which we can build this reinvention into our own practice: Carol Rodgers (2002) calls for objective, noninferential observation followed by complex analysis and experimentation. For the work and practice of a practical and busy teacher, I am content to define reflective practice less by the method and more by the intention.

Being a Critically Reflective Teacher

The most important factor in the inequality equation is the teacher. The teacher who can is the wedge driven between our students and the wall of imbalance.

In order to make sure that we are making responsible decisions for our schools and, even more importantly, not allowing our own internalized biased and harmful mindsets contribute to the very system we are working to dismantle, even the best intentioned teachers need to take stock of their own work. This effort needs to be frequent, robust, and ongoing.

There are many reasons for this. If our practice is not reflective and analyzed we are unable to appreciate the totality of what our students bring to the learning experience, resulting in the failure to leverage these qualities in the interest of their growth. H. Richard Milner (2003) tells us this:

> Race reflection does not necessarily involve a final destination; rather, it concerns conscious, effortful thinking that invites teachers to continually and persistently reflect on themselves as racial beings in order to better understand themselves in relation to others' racial identities, issues, and experiences and reject commonly held beliefs and stereotypes. (p. 176)

This practice must also look intentionally into the way race, class, gender, and power are manufactured in our classes. Milner (2003) goes on to tell us that "this reflection may be conceived as a process that naturally occurs, particularly where experienced teachers are concerned" (p. 176). Teachers who can must nurture the "skills and repertoire of knowledge" needed to effectively do this work. Even more pressing, we must recognize the importance and necessity of this habit. Even the most seasoned and well-meaning teachers need to actively walk this walk of an ongoing process.

And of course, why wouldn't we want to see our students and ourselves in our totality and our potential. Milner explains that the "Race reflection can be seen as a way to uncover inconspicuous beliefs, perceptions, and experiences, specifically where race is concerned. It can be a process to understand hidden values, dispositions, biases, and beliefs that were not in therefore of a teacher's thinking prior to conscious attempts to come to terms with them" (p. 175).

We reflect by making space to look at our work, both what we teach (our planning, instruction, and classroom environment) and what the students learn (often on the other side of a big gap between itself and our teaching). How you do this is up to you. My recommendation is that you build this habit into your existing routines. You can reflect by writing, by talking with your teaching community, while you are driving your car, brushing your teeth....

My reflection takes place most often when I am revising an existing activity or imagining new ways to cover familiar content. I think about student feedback (sometimes the most difficult part); I think about what was most meaningful and energetic for me—where the conversation thrived or languished, and most importantly, I integrate new perspective, ideas, strategies, and resources based on what happened before.

Without these new perspectives, points of view, resources, and strategies we aren't actually being critically reflective.

Freire calls this kind of reflection praxis. Praxis is a circular (or spiral or sometimes web-like) process of interrogating our action by imposing the theory.

This means: (1) we teach, (2) we think about our teaching and intersect that data with theory, (3) we deconstruct and reconstruct based on what we have taken from this process, and (4) we teach better.

But it isn't just to teach better, it is to teach better in a context of dismantling inequality and ensuring that our classrooms are our locations of change. Freire defines praxis in Pedagogy of the Oppressed as "reflection and action directed at the structures to be transformed" (p. 13).

What comes in the next chapter is an example of my own reflection around a small but significant time in my own teaching.

References

Dewey, J., & Boydston, J. A. (2008). The later works, 1925–1953: 3. Carbondale [u.a.: Southern Illinois Press.

Freire, P. (1972). *Pedagogy of the oppressed.* New York, NY: Herder and Herder.

Milner, H. R. (2003). Teacher reflection and race in cultural contexts: History, meanings, and methods in teaching. *Theory into Practice, 42*(3), 173–180.

Rodgers, C. (2002). Seeing student learning: Teacher change and the role of reflection. *Harvard Educational Review, 72*(2), 230–253.

· 1 0 ·

AN EXAMINATION OF MY OWN PRACTICE: A REFLECTION IN TWO PARTS

Chicago Catholic

> In this way the problem posing educator constantly re-forms his reflections in the reflection of the students. The students—no longer docile listeners—are now critical co-investigators in dialogue with the teacher.
>
> (Freire, 2000, p. 84)

In qualitative research, a testimonio is "developed by the one who testifies in the hope that his or her life's story will move the reader to action in concert with the group with which the testifier identifies" (Beverly, 2000, p. 540). The testimonio is a story told with an urgency to effect social change. This chapter is a testimony of my first years teaching, when I was often over my head and struggled sometimes just to make it to the end of the day. This chapter is an example of my own accountability. I recognize how difficult and challenging this process can be because I have been there myself. In the early days of my journey as a teacher, I often felt discouraged, hopeless, and that it was the students, not me, who were the problem. While I would never set up a teacher to believe, idealistically, that he or she will just love every single class they teach, it wasn't until connecting to critical pedagogy that I was able to see how much the internalized beliefs and fears I had about black children were driving the conflict in my classroom. Thankfully, I also felt empowered and driven to keep learning and to acquire more tools to help me navigate and unlearn some of the internalized ways of thinking I had learned about my students and myself.

Hence, the urgency of this testimony: So often, I see teachers engaging with power struggles with students and going home feeling validated in the notion that "these children" can't be taught. Rather than embarking on a process of uncovering the fears and low expectations, the difficult days just end up reinforcing all of the negativity and problems. This, coupled with the ridiculously high expectations of "saving the class from hell" that Hollywood proliferates, meaning that everyone is doomed from the beginning.

In an attempt to make myself as honest and vulnerable as possible, I am hoping that, in owning up to my own responsibility, I can encourage other teachers to take a difficult look at themselves in order to interrupt this process that is part of why schools become such a great place to maintain and nourish hegemony.

This chapter is also a critical-pedagogy "time capsule" of sorts. Having and keeping an examination of the culture and curriculum of one of the first schools where I taught provided me with the rare and unique opportunity to write a response and essentially look in the mirror at myself and my practice.

The first part of this chapter was written at the end of my second year at Chicago Catholic, and it was still the beginning of my journey into the world of critical pedagogy. While I had some insight into how the politics of race, gender roles, sexual orientation, and class impacted my day-to-day life, it is clear—to me, at least—that I had much to learn. I have not made any changes to this paper, which was written nearly seven years ago. The second part of this chapter is a reflection on my reflection and, because this is on ongoing process, the opportunity to take stock and learn more from a second vantage point.

Chicago Catholic High School is a small Catholic high school on the South Side of Chicago. For 38 years, the school has served African-American young men in the community. The school is extremely proud of the fact that for the last five years, 100% of the graduates have been accepted to college.

A typical day at Chicago Catholic High School would start before the first bell rings for class. Children were in the building at 6 a.m. Some of these boys were there for basketball practice; some were there because they lived far away and they just happened to arrive early; some were there because they didn't want to be anywhere else. In the mornings, before it was time to go into the school, they would sit in the lunchroom having breakfast, catching up, and playing cards. Then, at about 7:30, it would be time for them to get ready for class. I believe the most important word to use while describing Chicago Catholic would be "energy" because, at 7:30 in the morning, the students are already in full force, running everywhere, starting their days.

This energy sounded like music: their singing, their jokes, their laughter, their cursing, and their questions. By the end of the day, I and the other young women with whom I taught would lock ourselves in the women's bathroom and declare a "Chicago Catholic headache." The students would think this was funny because, apparently, they didn't give each other headaches.

This energy smelled like clean boys with their fabric softener and spray-starch shirts; like sweaty, funky boys fresh from the gym playing basketball, tumbling into my room after I just opened the windows and sprayed my powder-fresh air freshener (nothing too feminine…).

This energy looked like rows and rows of handsome young men with their round, brown heads, and their messy book bags, and their sunflower seeds, and their ties.

At 7:30, when the bell would ring, in came streams of boys in red sweaters. They would come with stories they had written, pictures of their older brothers' babies, books they wanted me to read, newspapers in which their writing had been published; their residual anger at their moms, or their sisters, or their grandmothers; bad news about family members who were in the hospital; runny noses; hurt fingers. And needing everything: safety pins, bus fare, lunch money, aspirin, little screws to hold their glasses together, birthday cards, everything.

A typical day at Chicago Catholic would include anger, disappointment, sadness, maybe a small scuffle, and, certainly, frustration. It would also include joy, celebration, friendship, family, and lots and lots of laughter. No matter where you looked in the building, you could always find a young man who was into something interesting and exciting and who would make you proud of him in that moment.

There was always a sense of family and community at Chicago Catholic. This was home, and this was where our family was. This feeling, along with all of that energy, usually made for a pretty good day. The young men supported each other; they worked together and they played together.

The building was small, and there were only about 350 students. This made it unusual to see a face that you didn't recognize. There was a sense of belonging and of safety. There are no metal detectors, and when the kids didn't feel well, they could rest in the principal's office. This is a home. A home where children learn, grow, play, and thrive. It is one of the last places in the country like this, one of the only schools dedicated to serving, preserving, and protecting African-American young men exclusively. This makes it a precious place and a place worth protecting.

Of course, it is easy to wax nostalgic about Chicago Catholic High School now—my visits to the school are affectionate and reminiscent—but there were bad days.

I have struggled with my own position in that school since my very first interview for a teaching position in the English Department. There were many questions that I struggled with, namely, the question of what it meant to teach in an all-male school. Should I have been using energy and these precious years of service to be working with young girls? How do I promote, or some days just maintain, my own sense of womanhood in a school whose mission statement was "Becoming Perfect Men?"

Eventually, I came to see that through teaching boys, through working with boys, I was indirectly working with the girls. This is how I came to strongly believe that there is no transformation in isolation. In order for young women to grow, the boys that populated their lives had to grow, too.

And there was much growing to be done.

When I was first hired, another young woman and I were the first young women to be hired at Chicago Catholic. The only other women who worked there were the English Department chair, who was the matriarch of the school and had been there for close to 20 years. There was one other female teacher, the college counselor, and the women who worked in the office. My first interviews were mostly about how I would control the boys and manage my classroom despite being a young woman who was smaller than most of the students and to whom the boys might be inclined to objectify. My response at all three interviews was that sometimes your best weapon could be a person's underestimation of you. I wasn't interested in whether or not the boys would objectify me—I was not the type of woman who would be thrown off by that—but I did know my subject, I was comfortable within a certain amount of chaos, and I felt that I had a lot to share with these students.

Still, I heard things like "They only hired you [and the other young teachers] so the men would have something to look at." This and countless other remarks like it made it difficult to negotiate my position in the school from day to day. In order for the boys to learn to relate with women in a professional manner, they needed practical experiences. This was the rationale the administration gave for wanting to hire young women. I wanted to teach. But I quickly learned that it would be impossible to remain neutral in a school that was so charged with gender issues.

Gender was not the only issue that defined the experience. The school is particular in many ways: the class, race, and gender population it serves; the fact that it is a Catholic, Franciscan institution; the goal and reality of getting every graduate admitted to college; and the fact that instructionally, the curriculum was not and still is not focused or unified were the defining factors for me.

The school was designed to serve African-American young men, so this is who the curriculum privileges. The mission of the school is "Becoming Perfect Men." Certainly, the school does its part to impart the values that make up perfect manhood to the students. Mass and the other rituals are a part of this. The boys are expected to behave and be polite and attentive during mass and prayer. This was my favorite time of day. It was peaceful, and I was surprised at how much I enjoyed the moments of reflection with the boys. If someone in the community was sick, we would be reminded to keep him in our thoughts. On Friday, we prayed the Peace Prayer of St. Francis, which states: "Where there is hatred let me bring love; where there is darkness, light; where there is doubt; hope…" and this prayer really did illuminate my time there. It reminded me about forgiveness and the unique roles we can play in one another's lives.

The trouble with "Becoming Perfect Men" is that it privileged the experience of the boys above all others. The notion was that they were an endangered species. This is a very dangerous message to put into the heads of teenage boys. First of all, it tells them that they are animals, reinforcing the very negative images they have to combat every day. Second, it absolves them. It accomplishes the opposite of what it is intended to do. Instead of giving them a sense of their self-worth and their worth within the community, and therefore the importance that they stay alive and make the most of their lives, it teaches them that they don't have to be accountable to themselves or to anyone else. If they are so precious, they should be able to get away with anything because to punish them might mean losing them, and that is a risk that we just can't afford to take.

The boys were very aware of this notion, as children will manage to pick up on and use any conflict in the structure of their lives to their advantage. And this notion was in conflict with many of the things that we attempted to teach the boys. These fractures in their world are where we lose children, not when we hold them accountable to their actions. When children feel that they can't count on the adults in their worlds to guide them with consistency, they turn to outside sources.

Single-sex schools have many advantages, but one of the drawbacks is that there is the lack of exposure to difference, and this is doubly so for Chicago Catholic. Mindsets about gender and race need to be constructed through experience and relationships so that the learner can empathize with the humanity of the other person. This is not always possible in an exclusive environment, and it could be exhausting to be one of the sole representatives of my entire gender.

No matter what, being a woman always positioned me as lesser in their eyes. The very act of being different from them equaled less to them. Any qualities that could be considered feminine, including asking for help or expressing any emotion (except anger at the loss of a basketball game), was considered less. My struggle became not to justify or defend who I was, but to change their whole perception of what was considered feminine. It meant different, but equal, not weaker. I wanted them to understand that all human beings had strengths and weaknesses. There were qualities we associate with being male and qualities that we associate with being female. One was not more valuable or more powerful than the other. The irony is that this is the same struggle they faced every day when they left Chicago Catholic and had to interact in a world that didn't privilege their situation. My hope was that by understanding themselves in relation to me, they might gain some insight into their relationship to the rest of the world.

The most difficult thing about being a teacher is the need to separate your nonteacher self from the image you project in the classroom in order to use yourself as an example, as text. This is a tremendously difficult and nebulous place to navigate sometimes, because while the boundaries of "teacher" and "student" are supposedly defined by the desk in front of the room, it is difficult not to personalize these roles; teachers are people, and students are people. This is true especially given the nature of what it really means to be a teacher, and the bizarre fact that perhaps no place else does the structure of the work deem it so necessary to maintain these roles and boundaries, despite their being so artificial and sometimes detrimental to the acts of teaching and learning.

The curriculum could have done a lot more to capitalize on the fact that the population was exclusive to African-American boys. It is not just about instilling pride in them because they are a unique extension of humanity, but also about teaching them to negotiate themselves in a larger, even global, community. If they feel empowered and valuable within this larger community, it will make it easier for them to understand what they contribute as individuals. While there is a curriculum of justice for them, there is not a curriculum of social justice for all, and I believe that the boys need to understand that if one person is oppressed, everyone is oppressed.

Catholicism

Since Chicago Catholic is a Catholic institution, this value system is what we tried to impart to the kids. For the most part, my experience with this was positive, and I believe this was the case for most of the students as well. The majority of the kids were not Catholic, but they seemed comfortable with the rituals and language of the religion. To me, the experience was more so marked with the presence of religion in the school, not just Catholicism in particular. This is a very pronounced difference for me when I visit Chicago Catholic after being in the public schools. In the public schools, any mention of God or spirituality is done so hesitantly and guiltily. While there is not a very strong presence of religious people at Chicago Catholic anymore—most of the staff is lay—there is still a freedom of religious expression. I think the real presence of Franciscan Catholicism in the curriculum is in the fact that the doors remain open to students even if they can't pay their tuition on time. In general, there is a sense of generosity and nurturing to the students that seems possible because of Franciscan values. While this is not exclusive to a Catholic school, it seems at least particular to Chicago Catholic.

College

College is a big part of the curriculum at Chicago Catholic. Getting the boys admitted to college was a big selling point for the school. I think that this message more than any other gave the boys, and the entire school, a sense of agency. If children are steeped, from the time they are freshmen, in the expectation that they will go to college, then chances are they will make it. It was not only about whether they would graduate from high school, but also that they would graduate from college, and everything would fall into place. I was not made aware of how strong of a message this was until I visited Chicago Catholic after leaving one of my schools. At Chicago Catholic there is a gigantic board announcing which child has been accepted to which school, and this board is not without its University of Illinois and Notre Dame acceptances. This is not the case with the other schools where I work. When I taught at Chicago Catholic, I wrote several letters of recommendation and helped to fill out many admission applications. I also hung many acceptance letters above my desk.

Of course, like all things, this program is not without its problems. Many of the boys go to college and don't make it. They are not adequately prepared, and they don't have support systems in place to help them adjust. However, I would strongly maintain that not helping them get accepted to college is not the solution to this problem. Some of the boys go and do quite well. I would, however, make the issue of preparedness and support something to be addressed and dealt with because setting a child up for failure is just as bad, if not worse, than not giving him or her a chance at all.

Instruction

There is weakness in the instructional program at Chicago Catholic for many reasons. Since it is not a public school, and therefore not accountable to a standardized assessment or any larger body, the program is not unified by any collective goal. The school has had to focus on keeping its doors open for the last decade, and the educational standards have slipped as a result of not being prioritized. The school is not strong enough to reap the benefits of the freedom associated with not having to worry about the test. This is a tragedy, because the uniqueness of the school's population and the freedom from the test could open up the doors to some very significant instructional possibilities. Lack of support and resources make these possibilities, not realities, for even the most talented teachers at Chicago Catholic. There needs to be unity and continuity in the curriculum so that what is happening freshman year is preparing students for their senior year and beyond.

Also, since it is a Catholic school, the teachers do not need to be certified or even have a background in education to teach there. The minimum requirement is a bachelor's degree. So while individuals may be talented in their field, they might not have a sense of the best pedagogical practice or even know what that means. Also, since the pay and resources are very low, the positions can sometimes attract unqualified people or young people (like myself) who simply can't afford to stay there and who move on after a couple of years. The school has a lot of turnover, and so it is difficult to get any sound instructional program to take root.

Nonetheless, I view this as a challenge. I think that there is tremendous instructional possibility at this school. The students are sophisticated enough to tackle a curriculum that would empower them through challenging them both politically and academically. They are aware enough to work within the curriculum to navigate and develop their own sense of identity and their position in the world. Since it is such a small school, a sense of community develops naturally with each new class. This, too, invites exciting instructional potential.

My experience at Chicago Catholic was, and continues to be, quite formative for me. I was able to navigate quite a bit for myself in terms of race, gender, and class through working there; I was, and continue to be, what Freire would call the learner and teacher. This is how I know what potential exists there. In fact, in retrospect, the possibility for learning and teaching is really how I would collectively define my time spent there.

A Reflection on My Reflection

Doing the work to examine our own practice: the successes and the mistakes can be uncomfortable, at best. But it is impossible to grow and exploit the benefits of growth without taking an honest look at where we once were.

I think I made several mistakes during my tenure at Chicago Catholic High School. I take some comfort in the belief that these mistakes were made because of ignorance that I have since taken great steps to overcome. I also take comfort in the belief that, ultimately, I did more good than harm. And certainly, the desire to do better has pushed me to confront and to learn. I have learned a tremendous amount from this experience. That is great for me, but I think less than great for my former students.

I started teaching, as most young teachers do, with a terrible combination of fear, arrogance, wanting to be liked, a need for validation, and the belief that connecting sentence structure to rap lyrics (a method that I had pioneered, of course) would get me through each day of a year that would end in my publishing a book with my students and me smiling—gangsta style—on the front cover.

As a biracial woman who was born in the city of Chicago but grew up in a predominantly white, poor, and very racist suburb, who was reemerging and reconnecting with African-American, urban culture, I was having my own kind of identity crisis. I was searching for validation and credibility, and kids can always pick up on this and run with it. This made it difficult to create the structure necessary to manage my classroom; this made it difficult for my more adventurous lessons to really succeed.

When my students didn't want to listen to the music I liked, got rambunctious or bored doing grammar lessons by writing comic books, I blamed them, not myself. And when they didn't see the connections I wanted them to make to The Bluest Eye (after all, Pecola Breedlove is oppressed; we're oppressed...), I got angry and impatient with them. It was tempting to say to myself, They don't want to learn; they are ungrateful. I realize now that even within a group of boys with the same age, racial and geographic background, there was no magic wand I could wave to instantly reach all of them. And regardless of what I was teaching, the best instruction required deliberate scaffolding to get each student from where they were to a new place.

Of course, most new teachers have similar stories, and through the passage of time, through practice and experience, confidence and competence are achieved. What is urgent about this testimony is how race, gender, and class shaped my expectations and played a part in where I started and I how I grew. And remember, they play a part for everyone. No one is exempt. This is just my particular journey.

Really, what I am most struck by, as I read and reread this paper, is what is missing. Where is the indignation about the mythology of the "endangered black male," the institutionalized fracturing of the African-American family, the gender inequity, the homophobia? I suppose it was there on many levels, and I can certainly trace its emergence over the years that would follow this experience.

Looking at the big picture, I take two very valuable lessons away from the experience. The first is that you cannot ignore the intrinsic complexity of the ways that the issues of class, race, and gender are played out in our schools and our lives.

The second is that hegemony and dominant culture are always present and pervasive. This means that it is entirely possible and, in fact, likely that you just don't see it. This also means that for the most part, issues that play out in oppressed communities are just hegemony and dominant culture pervading and maintaining itself: White people don't need to be present for whiteness to dominate. I initially thought that the curriculum privileged African-American boys, but I came to see later that this was not necessarily the case.

It is also important to note that my growth took place in different ways: in the form of personal confrontation and in looking at issues together with my students. It wasn't until later, after I had become more confident and grounded in my own practice and identity as a teacher, that the boys seemed less interested in challenging me and more interested in turning toward a question and trying to answer it together.

I had an early-childhood professor who told us that, regardless of parenting style, as long as you love the child and there is a general goodness-of-fit, you will be all right. I am satisfied that I did more good than harm because I did love my students, and there definitely was a strong goodness-of-fit. But in the years since, I have learned that not only is it not enough just to love them, but that pedagogy based on this belief is incredibly self-serving and arrogant. In fact, many researchers find that teachers' caring intentions may be misdirected, insufficient, and worse, replicate systems of inequality rather than interrupt them (Valenzuela, 1999).

Angela Valenzuela makes a distinction between aesthetic care and authentic care, or between schooling and education:

> ...schooling...is bound to institutional notions of success, including how well students perform on pre-determined, state-mandated curricula and standardized tests. This instrumental or results-driven approach to caring, also referred to as aesthetic caring (Valenzuela, 1999), often subtracts cultural and linguistic resources from students in the pursuit of academic achievement.

With this flawed approach when we teach without reflection and see our students in our own (often deficit and color blind terms) we are not seeing our students in their totality and potential. So, even if we care, our students may not be genuinely cared for at all.

With this setup, the teacher comes away feeling gratified and pleased with herself, and the student leaves short-changed. In any school, no matter the race or class of students being taught, it is not enough to love the students. Giving the students a quality education and empowering them to become self-advocates and productive members of their own families and communities is much more important. Ideally, this is done in a caring and loving environment, but that love must never, ever replace or substitute for excellence.

As with any developing teacher, I have drawn considerable boundaries since I first started teaching. Early in my career, I wanted to know all about my students' private lives; I wanted them to cry on my shoulder; I wanted to form lasting emotional bonds with them. This phenomenon becomes particularly true with younger students. Now I believe that this was more about what I needed than it was about what my students needed. When I see teachers do this now, I want to tell them: Be a great teacher, not an incomplete parent. While it is important, without doubt, that we care for and nurture our students, I believe that the best thing that we can do for them, especially the students with the greatest need for social support, is to teach them to be self-reliant and to have healthy, appropriate relationships with the people in their lives, people like teachers, who are there to support them. Give them a realistic sense of what they can expect and how they can learn to maximize those roles in their lives. In the long run, this also protects them from predators and people who will seek to use or victimize them because they are vulnerable.

This phenomenon may perhaps play itself out more so in urban schools, where the ratio of white teachers to students of color is especially high. Something I have seen repeatedly in my own experience is that young, white teachers who are just beginning their careers are still exploring and constructing their identities themselves. There is, of course, nothing wrong about this process. Yet the fluid quality of the teacher's own identity coupled with the excitement and curiosity of being in a new environment and community can naturally lead to a breaking down of boundaries.

The best that can come of this is wonderful: If teachers use this time to build themselves into human beings who are global and agents of bridge-building through relationships, they can go on to be a tremendous agent of change and living evidence of the power of schools to change power structures and dominant culture relationships. But if teachers don't do the work of truly examining their own issues with race and class, if they don't do the work of unpacking their own "knapsack," then the result can be a patriarchal colonization disguised as teaching that gets worse as the years progress—or worse, until the individual leaves the profession of teaching, after having "done their part," going back into their own communities to become heroes and bringing the myths of colonization with them. Students of color do not need surrogate parents; they need excellent teachers.

And yes, I am guilty of this myself. When I look back at the many ways the school failed the students academically and how as an instructional leader, I was implicit in that, I cringe.

I still have big questions, and I have ongoing conversations with my colleagues about whether or not we should consider African-American boys to be an "endangered species." I believe this thinking is problematic and either creates a false sense of entitlement or overburdens these boys, both undesirable outcomes. Complicating things even more, the boys often rejected this idea themselves, or at least failed to identify with the idea that they fit into this statistic somehow. Yet when one considers the statistics—one of four African-American men will at some point be tried in the legal justice system; there are more black men in prison than in college—it is difficult not to worry. As I have struggled with my family and one of the most important black men in my life, my brother, as he has had to deal with the reality of his own life and adult choices, it is difficult not to worry. This is an ongoing point of reflection for me and should be for any teacher, no matter who you teach. Everyone of this generation must consider these questions.

Another thing I struggle with is the question of college. Did we do these boys a disservice by sending them to college since they were unprepared and only come home after a semester having failed and lost a semester's tuition? While I believe that getting the students accepted to college is better than not, you can't ignore the long-term ramifications of going and not making it. I don't think the solution is not sending them. Rather, I believe it is import- ant to invest our time and energy in supporting programs that help students build community and support systems when they get to college. Such systems should be those that exist outside of fraternities and sororities—systems that encourage academic and long-term community success. I didn't counsel my students to join forces with any of these organizations, because I didn't know about them. This is just one more thing I didn't know. This reinforced for me the importance of knowing: of doing the research and building community so that I could better advocate for my students. In a larger sense, I see the importance of going to college, but even more, I see the importance of work- ing toward an economic reality where there is a choice and the alternative options still mean it is possible to live a solvent life and to care for your family and community because you work hard and contribute.

In the long run, I feel as though I resolved more of my own issues of gender than of race. I certainly learned about the parallels and the complexities of how these issues compound each other.

I think I resolved more of my personal issues, and I became a stronger woman and a more effective role model through this teaching experience. I have more answers about the issues of gender in education that I do about race. If anything at all came of my time at Chicago Catholic, it was the abil- ity to say this: If something is wrong, if you have done something wrong, my reaction is irrelevant. If you have done something disrespectful, or broken the rules, or broken a commitment you had with me, it doesn't matter if I sit here in stony silence, or if I go outside and do back flips. My reaction does not negate or negotiate your reaction. If you did something wrong, that belongs to you, and the burden is yours to fix it. Though I learned this through count-less conversations about missed assignments and late arrivals, in which the boys insisted I was "overreacting" or "trippin'," this lesson became increas-ingly important to me as I learned more about the relationship between the dominant culture and the oppressed. This is how a particular parallel between gender and race plays out.

It seems to me that for the burden to change, the fight always belongs to the oppressed, and that we seldom talk about the responsibility the dominant culture has to make change or how the dominant culture could benefit from making change (Sleeter & Grant, 1999). While the dominant culture cer-tainly benefits from exploitation of oppressed peoples, I believe there needs to be more conversation about how they can benefit from doing the opposite. In fact, the fight needs to become their fight as well. The endless conversations with the boys notwithstanding, this became a metaphor for me as I did more work as an educator and more work as a leader in schools. Recognizing that this is everyone's fight is especially important for teachers.

Truly, the most important thing I learned is how much more I had to learn. After having more "just teach your subject" conversations than I care to remember, I saw the importance of having a vocabulary, knowing theory, knowing theorists, and being able to cite historical and contemporary exam-ples that proved my case. The dominant culture has it easy: Their case is reinforced repeatedly through "normal" curriculum, through media, through just about every outlet there is. This means that we have to do three times the work to counteract their arguments and justifications for the reasons things are the way they are. I learned that I had a lot of work to do so that I could effectively and professionally advocate for the students I taught. This work is ongoing, and I am still both learner and teacher.

So, this is my example of looking at a moment of my own teaching through a critical lens. I want to demonstrate how the act of looking and the connection to theory can expand the potential for what we do and what we do next.

The nature of critical reflection can be an arduous task because it forces us to ask challenging questions that shape our construction of power and identity in our classrooms. Reflection is the antidote to being complicit in the oppres-sion of our students. While posing these questions proves difficult, honest answering of such questions becomes the bigger and more difficult hurdle to clear. Yet, the stakes are too high for teachers not to engage in this process.

References

Beverly, J. (2000). Testimonio, subalternity, and narrative authority. In N. K. Denzin & Y. S. Lincoln (Eds.), Handbook of qualitative research 9 (pp. 555–566). London & New Delhi: Sage Publications.

Freire, P. (2000). *Pedagogy of the oppressed*. New York, NY: Continuum.

Sleeter, C. E., & Grant, C. A. (1999). *Making choices for multicultural education*. Hoboken, NJ: John Wiley & Sons.

· 1 1 ·

PLANNING AND LEARNING—FROM COGNITION TO CULTURE

Liberating education consists of acts of cognition, not transferrals of information.
(Freire, 2000, p. 79)

Now that we have established that being a critical pedagogue requires a different approach to education and the work of schools, let's push further by looking at learning and teaching in order to connect the theory of critical pedagogy to our practice and methodology.

First, we will look at learning, specifically, cognition and the process of knowing. In order to unpack this process, we will look at theory that is established or mainstream in terms of its accepted application to all cultures; we will look at theory that is decentered, or that offers different approaches to learning and knowing; and we will look at how to connect these theories with our practice. This chapter is an interpretation of text, specifically, established educational theory of development, through the lens of critical pedagogy.

Cognition is knowing. It is both noun and verb: the act of knowing, the fact that one knows. It is knowledge. What cognition is is remarkably complex and, ironically, further complicated by attempts to define and understand it. How can something be the act of and the fact of at the same time? How can something be knowledge?

The attempt to define and speak of cognition is limited by the very borders of language itself. Because it is so complicated, maybe it becomes simple: Cognition is somehow everything at once—what one knows and how they know it.

Cognition is "the interaction of all of the perceptual, intellectual, and linguistic abilities that are involved in thinking and knowing" (Berger, 1994, p. 144). Janice Hale (1982) pushes this further, telling us that a "new direction of investigation suggests that cognition is social as well as biological. This new investigation direction looks at the relationship between one's culture and the kinds of cognitive skills one develops" (p. 23). It is at this point that we must make room for difference in order to effectively teach any child. In order to be effective educators, we must recognize the complicated existence of these places as well as the very involved factors that contribute to where these places are for our children on any given day, and how they arrived there as well. We must do this in order to respond to myriad ways in which these avenues manifest themselves through our children so that we can push them further every day.

Why seek to define cognition? Is cognition different from intelligence? Is it different from epistemology? From content? Is it also where these places intersect? If it is how our children perceive, think, and communicate, essentially how they continually organize and respond to their world, then we must understand cognition in order to structure their universe so that they can be taught at the most optimum levels possible. This means consciously constructing the environment in which they learn so as to be aware of and respond to everything—visual information, cultural information, emotional information, spatial information, the organization of time, and everything else imaginable.

Understanding cognition will help the educator anticipate what will happen as well as plan and create what he or she wants to happen, so that the children in the teacher's care can go as far as he or she knows they can go. However, the danger in seeking to define cognition is that the limitations of language itself may end up becoming devices with which the educator may inadvertently exclude or shortchange children because a particular child, and his or her own particular act of and fact of knowing, may not fit the definition. To define one act as somehow cognitively valid may automatically define another act as invalid, simply because of what it is not. This is why the educator must be aware of the many different ways that a child may know.

Because so much is so new and because, as the research of cognition will show us, children experience so many leaps and bounds as they develop, they are, in a sense, operating on much more active levels of cognition than the adults that teach them. So the educator must be aware of all that is happening, just so he or she can keep up.

This means careful planning. The teacher must consider cognition when setting goals, creating the physical environment, choosing reading material, assessing students' progress, and everything else that becomes a factor in the child's learning. Careful and deliberate consideration of these factors is a substantial job.

Fortunately, there is a world of thinkers who have provided us with landscapes, directions, and keys with which to navigate and chart courses. As we begin our journey, we will see that the work of two cognitive cartographers in particular, Jean Piaget and Lev Vygotsky, is essential.

Jean Piaget wasn't so much interested in education as he was in what he called genetic epistemology, the study of growth of knowledge in people. He began his own journey with observations of his own three children. His method, intense observation of small numbers of subjects, was different from what was considered valid in the U.S. at the time when he was working, and as we will see when we discuss Vygotsky, it had its own limitations. Nonetheless, it is fundamental to our understanding of education and development today.

Piaget's map is one of development—progress that is the result of the conflux of learning, experience, and maturation. The keys to his map are equilibrium and disequilibrium—the first being a state of balance, the second being what children experience when their balance is interrupted because new information has been introduced to their world.

He also gives us schemes and organization. Organization is the process of forming schemes, and schemes are patterns that describe how children perceive the world. Adaptation is the process of adjusting schemes to achieve and maintain equilibrium. Assimilation is when an existing scheme is changed in response to experience. Maturation is the biological change that occurs when a being interacts with the environment.

The landscape is organized into four stages: sensorimotor, preoperational, concrete operational, and formal operational. These stages develop continuously as a child is exposed to different experiences and opportunities. Understanding these stages helps us to see what a child is capable of as well as what kinds of learning experiences we can construct in order to help them maximize the space where they are.

What these stages also help us see is that cognition is different from intelligence, epistemology, or content because it seeks to define biological, universal stages that all human beings will encounter and work through (Eggen & Kauchak, 1997, pp. 27–47). In her book *Black Children*, Janice Hale (1982) takes an extensive look at the connection between cognition and culture. She tells us that African psychologists who are applying the work of Jean Piaget to the development of young African-American children find that "one of the reasons they look favorably upon Piaget's work is that the major aspects of his theory can be applied to all human societies and groups, and differences in performance can be accounted for without imputing inferiority and deficiency" (p. 24).

But what happens if a child progresses at a different rate or on a different route? Does he or she cease to develop; is the child no longer capable of reaching or flourishing in other stages? What if he or she is capable of more than what Piaget believed he or she should be capable of? And what happens to a child's development if he or she is exposed to different experiences and opportunities than were the small group of children that Piaget studied?

This is where we leave the territory of Piaget and meet up with Lev Vygotsky. He is the mapmaker who helps us understand the roles that culture and language play in how a child develops. He gives us a clearer picture of the linguistic, intellectual, and perceptual intersection and also takes us to the places where the child's inner, personal experience comes face to face with the complexities of the world in which he or she lives. Vygotsky gives us a sociocultural understanding of cognition that balances Piaget's biological, universal framework.

Vygotsky was taught through the Socratic method as a boy and later became a teacher himself. He believed the most important contributors to a child's development were language and social interactions.

Vygotsky's map is a map of zones that are navigated by language and constructed by scaffolding. He takes us to the place where language, social interaction, and activity intersect. The keys to his map are private speech; this is the metacognitive self-talk that guides thinking and action. There is the zone of proximal development, a range of tasks that a child cannot do by himself or herself but can accomplish with assistance. (This is, perhaps, halfway between equilibrium and disequilibrium.) Dynamic assessment is the observation of a child's ability within the context of a realistic problem. Shared understanding is achieved when both teacher and student have a common understanding of the task at hand. Scaffolding is the help the teacher gives that gets the child from one point to another point.

Vygotsky believed that cognition, what a child learns and how the child learns, was primarily social, and that "language provides learners with cognitive tools that allow them to think about the world and to solve problems." Vygotsky's map shows us that Piaget's schemes, in a large part, come from the culture that surrounds the child. While a child builds on these schemes to construct knowledge, he or she does so through interaction with others, not as an individual passive act (Eggen & Kauchak, 1997, pp. 47–56).

So now, considerations about content, environment, visual information, and organization of time become questions about moving a child from one zone to another, from disequilibrium to equilibrium, helping the child to develop schemes and to build on existing schemes, to share understanding and to scaffold. It is very clear that an awareness of cognition and a good map to guide the educator are crucial, and both of these mapmakers give us indispensable tools with which to work.

However, while we consider the limitations of Piaget's body of work, we must consider the implications of the space that is filled by Vygotsky's map, and the very primary role that culture plays in a child's cognitive development. It is the cultural component of the map that helps us to avoid the boundaries set down by language that may cause us to exclude a child's experience if it does not meet our expectations.

In *The Afrocentric Idea in Education*, Molefi Kete Asante (1991) asserts that "African Americans have been educated away from their own culture and traditions and attached to the fringes of European culture; thus dislocated from themselves." He believes that this is one of the "fundamental problems pertaining to the education of the African persons in America" (p. 289). If we are to follow the map that Vygotsky provides for us, then we must consider the culture of the child that we teach as well as the cognitive development.

Not only must we provide curriculum and standards that are developmentally appropriate for the child, but we must do so in the cultural language of the child as well. Learning and cognitive development are emotional experiences; therefore, we must seek to make our students comfortable and to feel that they belong. They must know that their experience is valid and important. If we don't do this, they will be unable to create the schemes necessary to engage in learning and we will be unable to create the scaffolds.

In her book *Black Children: Their Roots, Culture and Learning Styles*, Janice E. Hale (1982) tells us that if we do dislocate students from their culture, they experience "culture conflict." This can occur when a child may have a "storehouse of information, but it is not the background that is required for the school curriculum" (p. 39). As we would with any cultural group, we must consider the culture of African-American students when we are attempting to create scaffolds that will allow them to progress from one point to another as they move through the educational process.

The cultural conflict that exists in our schools today is tremendous, yet somehow we have become so accustomed to it that it has become invisible. In Chicago we have a number of schools that serve only African-American populations by design and a number of schools that do so by economic and geographic default. Yet the struggle to find resources that glorify or validate the children's experience, much less even come close to mirroring this distribution, is very difficult.

What does the culture of an African-American child look like? Whatever way we seek to define this, the first thing is that we must be sure that we are defining it through the strengths and not the weaknesses.

Traditional curriculum has taken us to a certain point, but beyond that, it has fallen short in terms of providing opportunities to teach through the use of the tools of one's culture and providing an "appropriate cultural foundation for all learners" (Watkins, 1993, p. 331). This involves creating ways for students to feel that what they are reading and learning is relevant to them. The teacher must create bridges or scaffolds in the classroom; "one important bridge is the effort made to relate the curriculum to the experiences and interests of students" (Sleeter & Grant, 1999, p. 56).

It would not be constructive or realistic to eliminate everything that we know and have worked with so far from the classroom or, certainly not, the standards and expectations that come with it. It is through the use of this canon that the standards and ideals of achievement that we work with have developed. We need a stable body of knowledge to draw from and to transmit to our students. But there are standards in nontraditional texts and tools as well. I am suggesting that the introduction to other, less traditional texts and tools, with a higher interest level, might dramatically increase learning on all levels.

It is fairly easy to find resources that promote the use of high-interest material in the classroom. What is not so easy is finding resources that promote African-American thinking and writing, especially rap or hip-hop lyrics, or anything associated with hip hop, as a useful tool in the classroom. But this is changing, especially as educators are becoming desperate for ways to connect with students and get them to read as we face a national decline in standardized test scores.

The cover of the March–April 2000 issue of Black Issues Book Review says, "Rap Is Poetry." In this article, canonized poets such as Sonia Sanchez are publicly endorsing hip hop as an important tool for use in our classrooms. "Possibly because of rap's commercial entertainment orientation, its coverage of such unsavory topics as criminality, drugs, and sex, and its authorship by a largely disenfranchised part of society, rap music has enjoyed little perceived intellectual currency" (Cook, 2000, p. 22). This has kept it out of the class-room. "Rap's economy, adherence to metaphor, simile, imagery and ability to express the pain and triumph of a people with an infectious cadence and an obsession with rhythm renders it poetry par excellence" (Cook, 2000, p. 27). Certainly, this is a much overlooked tool that if used effectively in the class-room could also help students connect to other material.

In the March–April 1999 issue of Black Issues Book Review, Jabari Asim writes that "the sociopolitical conditions of the present age, the growing black middle class, years of integrated schooling, and the sheer variety of black exis-tence in this country all contribute to an atmosphere in which newer writers feel comfortable following their own instincts." Clearly, this is something that English language-arts teachers should be capitalizing on and using as a tool to motivate our students (Asim, 1990, p. 25).

There is no doubt that our students must feel connected to the material they are learning in order to feel that they are participants in the classroom and their own learning. One of the most important things needed to create good study habits is the ability to establish a purpose for learning. Our stu-dents need reading they can relate to in order to have a starting point; from there they can become better readers and writers.

If we change what we value in the classroom, we can change what we value in the world. Won't our kids become better students if they feel that their experience and what is important to them are valued, both in the arena in which they learn and in the world into which they are emerging?

In order to empower our students to effect change in their own worlds, we must have as one of our goals for them to be self-aware and to have knowledge of their own history. In his Declaration of Rights of the Negro Peoples of the World, Marcus Garvey (1920) asserts that "the teaching in any school by alien teachers to our boys and girls, that the alien race is superior to the Negro race, is an insult to the Negro people of the world" (p. 28). This self-awareness develops from being steeped in a foundation that has empowerment as its base. Beyond this, there is the principle of Kujichagulia, or self-determination, one of the Seven Principles from the Nguzo Saba, developed by Maulana Karenga in the 1960s, which states that there should be the ability to "define ourselves, name ourselves, create for ourselves and speak for ourselves instead of being defined, named, created for and spoken for by others" (Karenga, 1998, p. 279).

When we are defined by others, especially those of a dominant, majority culture, it can only reinforce the idea that they hold a false superiority that does not exist.

This is certainly reflected by the typical reading list for a high school English classroom. The reading list for a Chicago high school that served only African-American males included 20 novels. Of these, only four were written by African-Americans. These lists typically include John Steinbeck, William Shakespeare, J. D. Salinger, George Orwell, and Ernest Hemingway. Furthermore, choices of novels that are supposed to represent African-Americans, such as I Know Why the Caged Bird Sings, by Maya Angelou, or Black Boy, by Richard Wright, often reinforce negative stereotypes of African-Americans being poor, abusive, and fragmented. Angelou tells the story of a little girl who is raped by an older, black male, and Wright's story is riddled with abuse and poverty. These books run the risk of validating already dangerous stereotypes. Unless these books are taught in a certain context, they do not define us, but instead speak disturbing untruths. Instead, we need to turn to the many offerings of literature that African-Americans have created that show us African-Americans in a positive, strong light.

In his book Cultural Literacy, E. D. Hirsch, Jr. (1987), a professor at the University of Virginia and a Senior Fellow of the National Endowment for the Humanities, offers a 63-page list of "What Every American Needs to Know." On this list of approximately 3,000 terms, fewer than 2% relate to African-American writers, historical achievements, or ideas. The majority of this 2% are athletes or fictional characters such as Uncle Tom (p. 211). This is significant because millions of copies of this book have sold. Along with other conservative educators, "Hirsch [has] sought to gain the upper hand in the debate over curriculum reform by reinvigorating the myth of Westerness and the role of Europe in the elaboration of American institutions and culture" (McCarthy & Crichlow, 1993, p. 294). The results of this line of thinking are the loss of countless opportunities for children to learn through their own process of self-determination, as well as a systemic cultural genocide through omission that will take place right in the classroom.

In order to sustain the goals of self-determination and critical thinking, as well as to create an environment where students can understand themselves, we need to acknowledge that the canon, as it exists now, is not aligned with these goals. Again, the idea is not to eliminate standards or expectations. Instead, we must create standards and expectations that emanate from a different source.

Malcolm X wrote *The Basic Unity Program* in 1965. In it, he proposes that Afro-Americans "write and publish the textbooks needed to liberate our minds" (p. 111). Around the same time, Nathan Hare, then the chairman of the San Francisco State College's Black Studies Department, called for a program with two phases—expressive and pragmatic. The first would "build in black youth a sense of pride or self, of collective destiny, a sense of pastness as a springboard in the quest for a new and better future" (Hare, 1969, p. 160). The second would instill skills that "can be directed at overcoming (or, if need be, overthrowing) his handicaps in dealing with his society" (Hare, 1969, p. 160). Clearly, while the fact that African-Americans currently score lower than European Americans on vocabulary, reading, and mathematics tests, as well as on tests that claim to measure scholastic aptitude and intelligence, which is only one of the challenges we face today, there is the need for some change. As long as an African-American male is more likely to end up dead or in prison than to go to college, there is the need for immediate change. I think this is simply stated by Jawanza Kunjufu (1990): "We have to improve our curriculum by making it multicultural, Afrocentric, and relevant" (p. 48).

These changes are necessary because all learning should seek to liberate its recipient from ignorance and powerlessness. If our students are empowered in the classroom, they can become agents of their own change. But without an explicit pedagogy, they will continue to be nonparticipants in their own learning, and they will continue to be held hostage by statistics and standardized-test scores. A revision of the curriculum means that the books students read in their classrooms would reflect their experiences. It would also mean that teachers must change their thinking to include their students' experiences. They must also move toward including text that reflects their students' experiences as valid classroom content. Changing would require letting go of the perspective that traditional curriculum is the only worthwhile material. This would mean the inclusion of hip-hop and rap lyrics by artists such as Lauren Hill and Mos Def in a poetry unit, not just as an example of "black poetry," but as examples of figurative language and imagery. This would mean the use of movies such as Friday, by Ice Cube, to illustrate conflict and characterization. It means elevating the importance of these works to the works of Hemingway and Steinbeck and making the effort to explain why. It means teaching our students that Malcolm X and Martin Luther King Jr. were, first, ordinary people, just like them, and that ordinary people can change the world, too. It would mean teaching history to reflect not only the greatness of Western civilization, but also the numerous and lasting contributions of the continent of Africa as well. If the typical cultural consideration afforded to a student in our schools is lacking and, worse, damaging, we can only assume that the cognitive implications will be tremendous.

I believe this calls for a dramatic unfolding of our maps as well as a serious revision of our curriculum, even changing what we consider to be culturally valid. This is a tremendous job for educators, but it is certainly worth it, considering how much we are failing our children and how much better deserving they are. Making the effort to connect the culture of school to the culture of our children will make it possible for us to maximize the tools that these educators have given us and to push our children even further than I am sure even they imagined.

References

Asante, M. K. (1991). The Afrocentric idea in education. In W. L. Van DeBurg (Ed.), *Modern black nationalism: From Marcus Garvey to Louis Farrakhan* (pp. 288–294). New York, NY: New York University Press.

Asim, J. (1990). Black poets for the new millennium. *Black Issues Book Review, 1,* 25–27.

Berger, K. S. (1994). *The developing person through the life span.* New York, NY: Worth Publishers.

Cook, D. (2000). The canonization of rap. *Black Issues Book Review,* 222–227.

Eggen, P., & Kauchak, D. (1997). *Educational psychology.* Upper Saddle River, NJ: Prentice Hall.

Freire, P. (2000). *Pedagogy of the oppressed.* New York, NY: Continuum.

Garvey, M. (1920). Declaration of rights of the Negro peoples of the world. In W. L. Van DeBurg (Ed.), *Modern black nationalism: From Marcus Garvey to Louis Farrakhan* (pp. 24–31). New York, NY: New York University Press.

Hale, J. E. (1982). *Black children: Their culture, roots and learning styles.* Baltimore, MD: John Hopkins Press.

Hare, N. (1969). Questions and answers about black students. In W. L. Van DeBurg (Ed.), *Modern black nationalism: From Marcus Garvey to Louis Farrakhan.* (pp. 158–174) New York, NY: New York University Press.

Hirsch, E. D., Jr. (1987). *Cultural literacy: What every American needs to know*. Boston, MA: Houghton Mifflin.

Karenga, M. (1998). From The Nguzo Saba (The Seven Principles): Their meaning and message. In W. L. Van DeBurg (Ed.), *Modern black nationalism: From Marcus Garvey to Louis Farrakhan* (pp. 276–287). New York, NY: New York University Press.

Kunjufu, J. (1990). *Countering the conspiracy to destroy black boys* (Vol. 3). Chicago, IL: African American Images.

McCarthy, C., & Crichlow, W. (Eds.). (1993). *Race, identity and representation in education*. New York, NY: Routledge.

Sleeter, C. E., & Grant, C. A. (1999). *Making choices for multicultural education*. Hoboken, NJ: John Wiley & Sons.

Watkins, W. H. (1993). Black curriculum orientation: A preliminary inquiry. *Harvard Educational Review, 63*, 321–337.

· 1 2 ·

TEACHING—THE PERFORMATIVE NATURE AND POTENTIAL OF CURRICULUM

There exists in curriculum development, and in teaching, something of a failure of nerve.

(Apple, 1990, p. 7)

What follows is an exploration of our teaching in relationship to critical pedagogy: Where do curriculum, assessment, and text intersect with critical pedagogy? How do we ask questions in a way that promotes critical thinking and dialogue? What can a reimagined, realized learning environment look like when critical theory is applied to our practice?

This chapter is an inquiry—specifically, writing as a method of inquiry. "Writing as a method of inquiry, then, provides a research practice through which we can investigate how we construct our world, ourselves, and others…" (Richardson, 2000, p. 925).

What Is Curriculum?

englishmathsciencechemistrylanguageartsreadingwritingphonicssocial
studieshistoryhumanitiesartliteraturereadingalgebratrigonometrygeometry
calculusstandardsobjectivesevaluationsactivitiesassignmentshomeworksub-
jectsgradesbookstextbooksbellsgymclassworkstandardizedtests

It's All Curriculum

All of the information the child receives, from all of his or her senses, from all of the room in the school, from every minute of the day, is curriculum. The teacher is curriculum. The teacher's words are curricula. Every interaction the child has, with text, with students: it is all curriculum. Curriculum has amazing and expansive power and influence in the lives of the children we teach. It is everywhere and at all times.

Knowledge is power. Those who have it are more powerful than those who do not. The people who define what counts as knowledge are the most powerful.

This means tremendous responsibility lies in the hands of the school and its teachers—and not only tremendous responsibility, but also tremendous potential. The location of transformation is the classroom. The classroom is where transformation lives, but it is also where transformation dies. Before this, one must recognize that the classroom is where acculturation lives and breathes. Historically, schools were "socialization factories, where it was hoped, 'American' values could be instilled into a diverse population" (Tozer, 2002, p. 49). This is aptly stated by Michael W. Apple in the book Ideology and Curriculum:

> For not only is there economic property, there also seems to be symbolic property—cultural capital—which schools preserve and distribute. Thus we can now get a more thorough understanding of how institutions of cultural preservation and distribution like schools create and recreate forms of consciousness that enable social control to be maintained without the necessity of dominant groups having to resort to overt mechanisms of domination. (Apple, 1990, p. 3)

If the school is trusted as the most significant location of implementing and governing the currency of social preservation, can it not also be entrusted with its undoing? The answer is evident, and the power of the classroom, the teacher, and the curriculum is inevitable. "I strongly argued that education was not a neutral enterprise, by the very nature of the institution, the educator was involved, whether he or she was conscious of it or not, in a political act" (Apple, 1990, p. 1). Embracing and exercising this power means first understanding the way that schools operate to preserve and distribute knowledge.

Who Do We Teach?

Virtually everyone. According to the U.S. Department of Education, enrollment in public elementary schools in this country is at 47 million children (2007). The population of these students represents virtually every country and every nation. Forty-two percent of these students are considered to be part of a minority group, and this is an increase of 20% points since 1972 (National Center for Educational Statistics, 2007).

What Do We Teach?

Despite the far-reaching and increasingly diverse population, there is a small group of textbook companies that provide educational resources to the schools across the country. The major publishing companies are Pearson, Prentice Hall, Houghton-Mifflin, McDougal Littell, McGraw Hill, and Glencoe. Furthermore, the textbook industry is heavily influenced by the largest states that spend the most money to put books in their schools. Consider that it is possible to regulate the political content of their texts, and publishers cannot afford to ignore those guidelines if they want to sell books. Texas, for example, is the second largest textbook market in the nation, spending upward of $50 million a year on schoolbooks. Any textbook used in the Texas schools must "promote citizenship and the understanding of the free enterprise system, emphasize patriotism and respect for recognized authority," according to the State Board of Education guidelines (Tozer, 1998, p. 273).

It can be considered even more disturbing that "private citizens oversee the Texas purchase each year to make sure that the guidelines are rigidly observed. Consequently, textbook publishers have tailored the contents of the books they sell throughout the nation in order not to offend Texan sensibilities" (Tozer, 1998, p. 273).

Beyond this, there are cultural critics such as E. D. Hirsch and Alan Bloom who believe that knowledge that is significant and relevant to the preservation of our country can be listed alphabetically and presented to our children as the authority and the truth. Never mind the fact that of the thousands of terms on the list, the names that refer to the African-American experience are mostly African countries or athletes.

According to this truth, the minorities who make up close to half of our country's school population have not made any significant contributions to our culture. At best, the contributions are derivative or marginalized. In order to deal with the infinity of differences that have been presented by the 47 million children we are teaching, anything that is different becomes substandard. Standardized tests only serve to validate this idea because the epistemology, cognition, and content evaluated with these tests can't possibly reflect the differences present in 47 million children.

How Do We Teach?

More and more, the shift is toward a standards-driven pedagogy that is supposed to close the gaps that exist among the different students in our public-school system, despite overwhelming evidence that these standards do nothing more than marginalize the groups of students who are left behind. In the ambitious No Child Left Behind Act (2002), our president vows to make it the mission of the public schools to "build the mind and character of every child, from every background, in every part of America" (The White House). Ironically, the principal tool in this operation is the standard, a measurement that should indicate where every child in the U.S., despite differences in background, should be at a certain point in their development. This plan will "insist that states set high standards for achievement in reading and math—the building blocks of all learning—and test every child in grades 3 through 9 to ensure that students are making progress" (The White House, 2007). This is a plan perhaps of the collective child, but certainly the individual child will be left behind.

This is because there is no standard child. According to FairTest: The National Center for Fair and Open Testing, "Standardized test are based on behaviorist theories from the nineteenth century. Today, cognitive and developmental psychologists understand that knowledge is not separable into bits and that people (including children) learn by connecting what they already know with what they are trying to learn" (FairTest, 2005). If we are attempting to teach 47 million children, each with different landscapes of strange and familiar, each with different landscapes of what they already know and what they are trying to learn, we cannot standardize knowledge and hope to truly teach. So curriculum becomes performative. Curriculum becomes the tool for creating the reality it describes.

What Is Performativity?

The performative nature and, consequently, the power of curriculum is that it simultaneously creates what it speaks. We have a concrete curriculum in this country, a body of knowledge of subjects and ideas that are privileged above all others and regarded as the truth. But we also have a more nebulous, abstract curriculum at work—what Michael Apple refers to as the hidden curriculum—the "tacit teaching of social and economic norms and expectations to students in schools" (Apple, 1990, p. 43). What happens in curriculum is the creation of a loop—where the concrete curriculum, by virtue of what it privileges and by what it excludes, performs itself, thus creating the hidden curriculum. In order to understand how performativity operates in education, we must understand education both as the verb—educating a child—and as the noun—the child's education. Education is both the process and the product.

How Is Education Performative?

Education becomes performative when certain concrete truths, such as the idea that Black English is substandard, are acted out through the process of educating a child instead of recognizing Black English as a complex and valid form of expression. Black English is regarded as incorrect, and therefore, the child who comes to kindergarten having spoken Black English all of his or her life is also incorrect. Considering the relationships that exist between language and identity, this rejection of the child because of the child's language, something he or she can barely separate from himself or herself, has huge implications. Gadamer tells us, "Learning to speak does not mean learning to use a preexistent tool for designating a world already somehow familiar to us; it means acquiring a familiarity and acquaintance with the world itself and how it confronts us" (1996, p. 79). This means that even the very initial experiences that the child has with school serve to negotiate and jeopardize his or her forming identity. If the hidden curriculum is to create a particular social and economic standing for this child, the concrete curriculum performs it.

When a language-arts curriculum operates with the notion that there is a canon of literature, a body of work that is supposed to encompass every universal human experience and speak to every member of the human audience, it creates this truth that it speaks. If the canon privileges the voice of white patriarchy by employing only the voices of white males—Ernest Hemingway,

F. Scott Fitzgerald, John Steinbeck—and places all other voices on the periph-ery, insisting that they are valid only in relation to the dominant voice, it cre-ates the truth it speaks. It does this by ensuring that students will be exposed only to that voice and that they will come to understand that voice as the only valid voice, even if it means becoming increasingly uncomfortable with their own voice or stories that speak to their own experience. By excluding the cultural contributions of entire races of people in this country, the literary canon continues not only to define the genre, but also to decide who can create what, and it defines the creations of others as well.

When an educational reform act proposes to leave no child behind and promises to do so by standardizing knowledge and then testing every child from third to eighth grade on this knowledge, it seeks to legitimatize only one way of knowing, only one way of understanding, and only one body of knowledge, and it does so to the exclusion of everything and everyone else. The fact that minority students continue to perform lower on standardized tests than do their white counterparts is not just a random correspondence. This fact in itself is performative, in that this idea helps to shape the way minority students and their potential are viewed in this country.

How does understanding the performativity of curriculum help to inform our teaching? In her book *Teaching to Transgress*, bell hooks (1984) tells us that when we as educators allow our pedagogy to be radically changed by our recognition of a multicultural world, we can give students the education they desire and deserve. We can teach in ways that transform consciousness, creating a climate of free expression that is the essence of a truly liberatory education (p. 39).

If the classroom and the curriculum are capable of producing and per-forming on curriculum, can they not also be responsible for undoing that cur-riculum and reinstating a new one? And if this will not take place in the classroom, then where?

Understanding the performativity of the curriculum means questioning and reflecting upon each moment in the classroom, not only upon the imme-diate transmission of what we are teaching, but pushing further to question what the ideas will do to form the child's identity, ideology, and interaction with the world. It means questioning our evaluative processes and seeing these processes as a potentially formative act as well as an act of assessment. It means being aware and conscious of teaching as a political act, and taking responsibility for this act and this process.

References

Apple, M. W. (1990). *Ideology and curriculum*. New York, NY: Routledge.

FairTest: The National Center for Fair & Open Testing. (2005). *How standardized testing damages education*. Retrieved February 18, 2004 from http://www.fairtest.org/facts/howharm.htm

Gadamer, H. (1996). *The enigma of health*. Stanford, CA: Stanford University Press.

hooks, b. (1994). Teaching to transgress. New York: Routledge.

Richardson, L. (2000). Writing: A method of inquiry. In N. K. Denzin & Y. S. Lincoln (Eds.), *Handbook of qualitative research* (pp. 923–948). London & New Delhi: Sage Publications.

Tozer, S. (2002). *School and society: Historical and contemporary perspectives*. Boston, MA: McGraw-Hill.

White House, The. President Bush signs landmark education reforms into law. Retrieved November 14, 2006, from http://www.whitehouse.gov/infocus/education/

· 1 3 ·

TEACHING—LOOKING AT TEXT

The Simpsons and The Bluest Eye

Indeed, even the inclusion of such "classics" as Shakespeare within the curriculum of schools in the United States came about only after prolonged and intense battles, ones that were the equal of the divisive debates over whose knowledge should be taught today.

(Apple, 2001, p. 49)

There are many benefits to using the Simpsons in classes. The obvious is that it's funny. Laughing students are not sleeping students. The fact that students will already know the show—and that we can then use the show as a jumping off point for their lessons—is beyond helpful. Students may be at first resistant to seeing the familiar as strange, which is required for critical thinking, but they become engaged when they are able to use their familiarity with a subject as knowledge. They are already experts on their culture: why not let them use their strengths as we take them into an unfamiliar realm of discourse: Karma Waltonen and Denise Du Vernay.

These chapters also interrogate and interpret text; however, this time the question is how can we deconstruct, reappropriate, and redefine text in order to create a more deeply engaging curriculum. I am looking at the Simpsons because this show is pervasive and exhaustive. The show has, at one time or another, for better or worse, covered nearly every facet and aspect of American culture. In addition to being a dense source of prior knowledge upon which we can scaffold new learning (funds of knowledge), the Simpsons can also have the benefit of "shared experience for students, allowing them to interact with other youth" or share what Moje calls peer funds. This can go toward helping them to see themselves in an immediate and broader cultural context. Even more, Moje describes "The popular cultural text…serve(s) as a mediator for the print text." And that, "The Simpsons episode also seemed to give the print text some credibility or worth" (Moje et al., 2004, p. 65). That's great, right??

This is meant to be descriptive, not prescriptive. I am not necessarily recommending the Simpsons, but instead saying, bringing popular culture into the classroom is a pretty good idea, so when you decide to do this, here is one way to think about it.

The Simpsons

"You are Lisa Simpson."
—Mr. Bergstrom, Lisa's substitute teacher, on The Simpsons

(Groening, 1990)

I argued strongly that education was not a neutral enterprise, that by the very nature of the institution, the educator was involved, whether he or she was conscious of it or not, in a political act.

(Apple, 1990, p. 1)

If Apple is correct, then the question becomes, what do we do? What can the conscious teacher do to ensure that his or her involvement in this political act is positive and not detrimental to his or her students or career? What tools and avenues does the teacher have?

One thing the teacher has is the content of the curriculum he or she presents to the students. This means having the courage and the insight, as well as the mastery of the subject, to look in unexpected places for content and curriculum and for resources to use in the classroom. This also means, more importantly, to explode the traditional limits of what is considered curriculum and to begin to treat the whole world as text. A child who has the skills to decode his or her whole world as text will have the skills to negotiate standardized tests and any other standardized challenge the child faces.

The keys are connection and motivation. There is no magic to the idea that a student needs to feel involved and engaged with what he or she is learning.

This is true at even the highest levels of academia. If we meet the students where they are, we can use that point as a beginning and use the connection to establish links between where they are and where we want them to be.

Pop culture, their culture, is a tool. The question that educators should be asking is not what is it doing to our children, but what are we doing with it? There is a multitude of resources in their world. We need to build a language and a map with which to navigate it. We need to take their worlds seriously and make use of them.

There is a rich history of the subversive being couched in the seemingly innocent world of children's culture. The worlds of make-believe places have many secret hiding places. The fairy tales of the Brothers Grimm and Hans Christian Andersen inhabit universes that are rich with subtext and symbolism. The characters are constantly defying authority. The worlds, which are generally violent, tragic, abusive places, constantly shift and remake themselves. For generations, poets and writers have borrowed from the world of fairy tales, and this is not without reason: They help us understand the nature of our own worlds, "to learn not only about our inner fantasies but also about our outer realities" (Luthi, 1976, p. 1).

Perhaps building on tradition, children's classics such as Alice and Wonderland and The Wizard of Oz, along with the infinite and wonderful world of Disney, are also brimming with hidden curricula that are thinly masked as innocent child's play.

Alice in Wonderland is laden with astounding symbolic meaning, a "mathematical logic...and a profound psychological perception underlying the fantasy" (Wallace & Wallechinsky, 1978, p. 836). The characters in this story range from the Queen of Hearts, a castrating, dominating queen with a timid king, to the Mad Hatter, who is based on the felt-hat makers of old England who used mercury to treat the wool and eventually suffered brain damage from the poisoning (Wallace & Wallechinsky, 1978). Certainly, there are plenty of opportunities for critical-thinking skills to be challenged with a story like this.

Writers such as Henry B. Littlefield, who wrote The Wizard of Oz: Parable on Populism, and Osmand Beckwith, author of The Oddness of Oz, believed that The Wizard of Oz was really veiled propaganda for the Populist Movement. Baum was a Populist, and there are theories that the story is really an allegorical reconstruction of the political environment during the late 1800s (Bencruiscutto, personal communication, April 18, 1996).

Today, one of the most popular television shows is The Simpsons. Started in 1987, The Simpsons is one of the longest-running prime-time television shows and has been consistently one of the Fox TV network's most popular shows.

This show deconstructs all that television holds dear: the nuclear family, the public-school system, the political process, and the workplace. All the while, it pushes every stereotype to the point of destroying them.

This family is like the average family: They fight, they struggle. Critics think that Bart Simpson and the rest of his yellow family members are a bad influence on children and society, that, perhaps, they make the American family look bad. Newsweek refers to them in a cover story as "TV's newest domestic travesty" (Waters, 1990, p. 60).

On the surface, it seems they promote a poisonous set of values: defiance of authority and the questioning of every institution that supposedly holds this country intact. Yet the irony is that this family actually supports a very strong sense of family values. They support one another, they communicate, they struggle to stay together despite their differences with each other and with the outside world. They believe in one another, and they love each other.

In the episode "Bart Goes to Military School," when his parents have reached their limit of tolerance with his social deviance, they decide to send him to military school. Lisa decides to stay after seeing the level of educational standards in a class that reads poetry and recites Keats: "Truth is beauty, beauty truth, Sir!"

After being hazed, harassed, and ostracized, the final test is when she must climb the Eliminator, a 50-foot rope that is suspended over thorny patches of weeds. Her brother sneaks out of his bunk to help train her, despite the risk that he may be found supporting the "girl issue." At the end, when she is still unable to make it across, he steps forward and cheers her on despite the rest of the boys booing her. She makes it across because her brother believed that she could. She has the courage to climb the rope because he had the courage to step forward and support her.

How many families can claim all that?

The public-school system is a common target for criticism. The elementary school that Bart and Lisa both attend is run by an inept principal who has no idea about the daily happenings in his school, and staffed with teachers who can't teach a lesson without their Teacher's editions. Lisa is consistently underchallenged, while Bart gets away with everything and practically runs the school himself. School is set up on this television show as a place that inhibits freedom, individuality, and critical thinking. In one of the yearly Halloween episodes, when Lisa questions the origin of one of the dishes the cafeteria is serving, the lunch lady (who is also the school nurse) reaches beneath her table and pushes a "free-thinking alarm."

Lisa goes into a very uncharacteristic depression when the results of a standardized test she has taken position her as a future housewife. Her hopes and dreams of becoming the future Nobel Prize–winning President of the United States are squashed. She retaliates by cheating on homework and tests and, in a final act of defiance, desecrating the school mascot. The message remains clear, however, that it is possible to maintain individuality and transcend the limitations that school places on spirit and individuality.

The magic of this show is that it accomplishes what often can be so impossible in the classroom. It gives students the prompts and the opportunities to identify with an interrupter. Bart is trouble "but only at school- a place he finds boring, confining, and based on a childhood that no longer exists." (Kincheloe, 2004, p. 48). We are told, "Bart is not childish, the school is." (p. 48)

In the episode "Lisa's Substitute," when Lisa's regular teacher has to take a medical leave due to a psychosomatic bout with Lyme disease, Lisa finds herself developing a crush on her substitute, Mr. Bergstrom. He teaches the children through experiential learning, making a lesson out of each child displaying a talent that is unique to them, and giving them assignments such as bringing in one indigenous rock from the playground in order to enter the classroom after recess. When Lisa is feeling discouraged and alienated because of her brother's involvement in a race for class president that is really just a popularity contest, Mr. Bergstrom encourages her with assurance that one day she will be in a place where "her intelligence is an asset and not a liability."

When the regular teacher returns, she asks the class what on earth he taught them because he didn't touch her lesson plans. Lisa's response is "That life is worth living."

They say goodbye to each other right before he boards the train to work in the projects of Capital City. When Lisa asks him how he could leave her, he tells her, "That is the problem with being middle-class; anybody who really cares will abandon you for those who need it more." He hands her a note that says "You are Lisa Simpson" and tells her, "Whenever you feel like you're alone and there is nobody you can rely on, this is all you need to know."

The message that appears is that learning is experiential. It is about relationships and connections that we make because we care about who and what is involved. It is, as John Dewey says, a "process [that] has two sides—one psychological and one sociological" (1959, p. 20).

When Homer's boss, the cantankerous Mr. Burns, owner of the local nuclear-power plant, tries to buy an election, the political process becomes grist for the ideological mill. Marge Simpson, the matriarch and the murmuring voice of what is rational and right, agrees to serve Mr. Burns dinner at their home in order to create a photo opportunity because he is being perceived by the public as being out of touch with the common people. Lisa is doubtful, and she becomes even more skeptical after being asked to read a prescribed question from an index card for the camera. Her mother tells Lisa to trust her, and much to the dismay of Mr. Burns' makeup artists and spin doctors, she serves Mr. Burns a three-eyed mutated fish from the local reservoir, the very reservoir that has been polluted with nuclear waste from Mr. Burns' power plant.

This is one of the many episodes that criticize the political process. The Presidents are not immune; one episode even characterized Bob Dole and Bill Clinton as aliens. When the aliens agree to work together, they eliminate the problem of being from different parties, saying they are both the same anyway. Why is this important? Many television shows parody our political process and our leaders. It is important because resources designed for children to understand the political process do not assume that children are sophisticated enough to understand this kind of satire. The fact that the show assumes this level of sophistication on the part of its audience at all sets it apart from just about all children's television and, unfortunately, just about all classroom resources as well.

Certainly, the show presents one point of view. While this point of view may not be the one espoused by all classroom teachers, what is important is that the show can be an opportunity to introduce these ideas to a classroom in a way that is both palatable and manageable to the students. This calls upon the political act that Michael Apple refers to, and it gives the teacher an opportunity to help his or her students shape their own political position. Even better, it does so in a way that will be entertaining to students and therefore engaging. One does not have to worry about compromising the integrity of the text used in class or losing sight of instructional priorities, because The Simpsons is just a prime-time television cartoon. The show consistently makes reference to a wide variety of texts, documents, political and cultural figures, and both national and global historical events. It would be easy to make a transition from the show to the actual source while it is still relevant to the children.

The world of work is possibly the place that catches the closest look from the critical eye of the show's creators. Work is metaphor for conformity and the hegemonic strongholds that dominate the world that surrounds the little box that sits in all of our living rooms. Homer, the patriarch of the family, takes little pride in his job and does as little as possible, but he also never misses an opportunity to "kiss up" to his boss. His boss, Mr. Burns, is the most powerful symbol in the small town of Springfield, where they reside. He is the man. He is the embodiment of corporate indifference and domination. In the episode "Who Shot Mr. Burns," when he is found with a bullet in his chest, the entire town is suspected of pulling the trigger. Homer is quickly narrowed down as the primary suspect because of a previous attack on Mr. Burns at the nuclear-power plant.

Frustrated because Mr. Burns has repeatedly forgotten his name, Homer spray-paints I AM HOMER SIMPSON on the wall in Mr. Burns' office at the plant. When Mr. Burns still can't remember his name, Homer attacks him, shouting, "Say it! I am Homer Simpson!" This is a very large statement about the struggle to maintain identity in the overpowering world of social, economic, and cultural control.

At first glance, it may seem as though The Simpsons is guilty of stereotyping. The owner of the "Quicky Mart" is Apu Nahasapamapitapetilan, who is from India. The town's doctor is an African-American man obviously based on Bill Cosby, who has had every stereotypical African-American hairstyle, from braids to an afro, even a Mr. T mohawk. When the family goes to eat sushi for the first time, Homer nearly dies because he has eaten a poisonous blowfish that was not prepared the right way. In fact, any group or individual that is featured on the show is treated as a stereotype, as a flat image with everything that we expect to see served right up. How do they get away with this? They do because the most stereotyped characters on the show are the Simpsons themselves. They are white, live in a house with two cars, a cat, a dog, and 3.2 kids. They are the biggest targets. But beyond this, they get away with it because the very fact that stereotypes are so conspicuous makes them the antithesis of themselves. The show's reliance on the sophistication of its audience makes it possible to do this in a way that is instructive and not offensive.

So how does the conscious teacher use this as a tool in the classroom? What kind of educational resource is the show? The show can be a way to scaffold information for children. Virtually every topic imaginable is a subject or a reference in The Simpsons: Modern art, Bible stories, jazz music,

World War II, the films of Stanley Kubrick, the electoral process, the poetry of Edgar Allen Poe, the novels of Charles Dickens, the Australian ecosystem, violence in children's cartoons, child abuse, and police brutality are just a few. The situations that are set up on The Simpsons provide endless resources for writing prompts and ways to engage critical thinking skills. The teacher would be limited only to his or her own imagination. I would argue that an episode of The Simpsons is as solid a resource as any short story in any typical classroom textbook. As stated earlier, the show can also be leveraged as a tool for accessing print media. You can use the show to demonstrate elements of literature: character, theme, conflict, symbolism. Even more straightforward, you can use the show to prompt writing subjects from family dynamics, gender construction, the justice system, corporate greed, or the role of schooling in our lives.

Of course, I am not suggesting that it would make sense to replace textbooks with a 22-minute cartoon. What I am suggesting is that one way to negotiate our role in this political process is to rethink what we consider to be curriculum and content and make some room for the tools of their culture: the culture of our students. They need to know that their culture is important, both historically and immediately. They also need to see that it has context. I hope that if we can do this, we can teach them to think critically and deeply about their own culture and about the whole world. As they emerge as individuals and as products of this political culture, they should have the ability to see the whole world as text, and themselves as a meaningful and empowered part of it.

Teaching for Empathy and Connection: Toni Morrison—The Bluest Eye

"Morrison often does the unthinkable as a minority, as a woman, as a former member of the working class: She democratically opens the door to all of her books only to say, 'You can come in and you can sit, and you can tell me what you think, and I'm glad you are here, but you should know that this house isn't built for you or by you.'" Here, blackness isn't a commodity; it isn't inherently political; it is the race of a people who are varied and complicated. This is where her works become less of a history and more of a liturgy, still stretching across geographies and time, but now more pointedly, to capture and historicize: This is how we pray, this is how we escape, this is how we hurt, this is how we repent, this is how we move on. It is a project that, although ignored by many critics, evidences itself on the page. It has allowed Morrison to play with language, to take chances with how stories unravel and to consistently resist the demand to create an empirical understanding of black life in America. Instead, she makes black life—regular, quotidian black life, the kind that doesn't sell out concert halls or sports stadiums—complex, fantastic and heroic, despite its devaluation.

The Radical Vision of Toni Morrison By Rachel Kaadzi Ghansah "But since why is difficult to handle, one must take refuge in how" (Morrison, 2000, p. 7).

Let us take refuge in how. We will make it our jobs, our work to understand completely the how. We will learn it, memorize it, standardize it—and then undo it. The first and possibly most painful step to learning the how is recognizing the role that education has played in constructing and reproducing it. Faced with the daunting tasks of teaching (for a lot less money than they deserve), without enough resources, children who are not motivated and most likely have several other more pressing needs, in buildings that are inadequate and run down—and always with the pressure of the next standardized test weighing in—the last thing most teachers want to deal with, much less take responsibility for, is the how. But it is inevitable. Ultimately understanding the how will help to inform our work and better understand and serve our schools and our students. According to Michael Apple (1990):

> One of our basic problems as educators and as political beings is to begin to grapple with the ways of understanding how the kinds of cultural resources and symbols schools select and organize are dialectically related to the kinds of normative and conceptual consciousness "required" by a stratified society. (p. 2)

This is the most basic problem. Once we begin to grapple with this, we find that persistent and overwhelming problems that manifest themselves in our classrooms as immediate, day-to-day problems are often rooted in complicated places. What is also implied in Apple's quote is that as a nation, we have been individually divorced from our own truths, our own stories and narratives, so that we could collectively participate in this conceptual consciousness. It becomes easier and easier to connect the basic curriculum and the agenda of standardization and test-taking to the cultural resources and symbols of which Apple speaks. In fact, it becomes more than easy if the agenda of stratification is couched in the rhetoric of standardization and achievement and accountability. Who can argue with the notion of "no child left behind?" I don't want the children that I teach to be left behind. And so—just like that—in order to keep up, you must stratify. And certainly through history this has been no different. In fact, Apple also reminds us that one of the curriculum field's most important early members, Franklin Bobbit, helped to shape our field today because he saw the curriculum as one means to develop what he called large group consciousness, his term for the individual's feeling of belonging to his or her social and economic group or community and that individual's commitment to its ends, values, and standards of behavior (Apple, 1990, p. 69).

But why is it necessary to understand how this came to be? In her study entitled How White Teachers Construct Race, Christine Sleeter and Grant (1999) speak of the experiences white teachers had when teaching black children about Africa as part of a unit on family heritage:

> At times African American students resisted participating in lessons about ethnic origins, and this puzzled the teachers. For example, a teacher who taught a lesson remarked that ...one little boy said "we didn't come from Africa." When another teacher began a lesson with a discussion of where students' ancestors came from, she was similarly surprised that no African American students located their ancestry in Africa. (p. 166)

Why is it necessary? Because we forget. Because it becomes invisible, and the maintenance and reproduction of the how depends and thrives on forgetting and invisibility. Does remembering apply only to those who teach black children? No; in fact, it is even more important to recognize and insist on the understanding that the educational experience for black children in this country is a metaphor for the teaching of all children in this country. Beyond that, there is no transformation in isolation. The child who is taught to benefit from the curriculum of hegemony and white privilege exists in as much of a ghetto as any other child. We must expand our collective conceptual consciousness to include both sides.

So, what do we find if we draw the curtain? Consider the teaching of literature.

First, consider that Jacques Derrida, quoted in Derrida for Beginners, (1980) tells us that within literature, one can make the most powerful political statements, because essentially, within literature, one can say anything (p. 5).

Jerome S. Bruner (1994) asks, "If it is granted, for example, that it is desirable to give children an awareness of the meaning of human tragedy and a sense of compassion for it, is it not possible at the earliest appropriate age to teach the literature of tragedy in a manner that illuminates but does not threaten?" (p. 360). Furthermore, he states that:

> The high school student reading Moby Dick can only understand more deeply if he can be led to understand that Melville's novel is, among other things, a study of the theme of evil and the plight of those pursuing this "killer whale." And if the student is

led to further understand that there are a relatively limited number of human plights about which novels are written, he understands literature the better for it. (p. 360)

Now consider Toni Morrison's The Bluest Eye (2000). As political text, as an explication of a human plight, the novel accomplishes so much. Because of literary merit alone, the Nobel Prize–winning novel stands beside itself in its ability to construct symbol and metaphor; to create characters whose voices we can hear whispering in our ears; to paint images of a fragile, small town; to capture the perspective of a little girl. Beyond this, the novel asks us to confront some more challenging and painful questions. What can we learn from children? What can a child bear to know? How do we collectively and as individuals construct identity? How do we arrive at our own understanding of reality? How is it that we come to know? How is it that one knowledge gets to be superior to another? What happens to a child who is not sufficiently loved, guided, and recognized? What does the product of racism and hatred actually look like?

Because there is no understanding of the U.S. without understanding racism and hatred, because there is no understanding family without understanding love and the knowledge possessed by children, because there is no understanding humanity without understanding the basic construction of identity—Morrison manages to achieve that which is virtually impossible. She pulls back the curtain on the invisible. She exposes the photo-negative of the American dream. She takes the experience of the other—of the invisible—and she raises it to the universal. This novel is important to everyone. These questions are not specific to the black experience. So the purpose of the novel becomes twofold: exposure of the brutality and infinite power of racism and poverty (holding everyone accountable), and then translation of this experience from a primarily black experience to a universal one.

Morrison herself stated that her intent was to "take love and the effects of the scarcity in the world as her major themes…to show us how to survive whole in a world where we are all of us, in some measure, victims of something" (www.Allian-Morrison.com).

The Bluest Eye is the story of Pecola Breedlove, a small, poor, black child who is the most helpless and unfortunate victim of racism and cruelty. She begins to think that if only she possessed the symbolic qualities of whiteness, beginning with an obsession with Shirley Temple, she would be absolved of her misery. Eventually she is given the blue eyes—from a "faith healer" named Soaphead Church—and she believes herself to be delivered. What has really happened is Pecola's break with reality, a result of the brutal chain of events to which she falls victim, ending with her losing her child—the product of her father's raping her.

The beauty of Morrison's novel is balance. The Bluest Eye is also the story of Claudia MacTeer, part of the MacTeer family, who temporarily takes Pecola in after a particularly bad run-in in the Breedlove household. Where there is chaos in the Breedlove household, there is structure in the MacTeer household. Pecola is raped by her father and consequently beaten by her mother because the woman thinks that Pecola is to blame; but when Frieda, Claudia's sister, is attacked by one of the family's boarders, Mr. Henry, their father, confronts him violently in broad view for all to see.

Perhaps what Morrison is able to create is ultimately a vision of the American dream—both sides of it—that is not as simple as it seems. This, too, is a universal theme. No stone is left unturned. She speaks of the racism that black people inflict upon other blacks; indeed, most of the worst cruelty that Pecola suffers is at the hands of black people in her community. She speaks to the horrors that black men inflict upon black women; she speaks to the fact that blacks are often accessories to crime committed against blacks, both in the home and on the playground.

Teaching the Bluest Eye gives us the opportunity to explore the narrative of what belongs in the canon and who gets to make those choices. It makes a space for us to think about representation, whose stories are typically represented, what happens when there are few opportunities to identify with the characters we read about and even more, what happens when we are given the chance to identify and empathize with someone so different from ourselves.

While she exposes all of these questions, she never once lets us forget that there is a true source for this hatred and tragedy. It is the same racism that is acted out through the Breedloves, father, mother, and child, and through the MacTeers—and all of the rest of the characters that inhabit this book as well. The most important thing that this does is to bring things to light. The story that the novel unfolds is a story that everyone needs to hear, and this is because it is ultimately everyone's story. She connects us back to our own truth.

References

Apple, M. W. (1990). Ideology and curriculum. New York, NY: Routledge.
Beckwith, O. (1976). The oddness of oz. Children's Literature, 5, 74–91.

Bencruiscutto, B. (1996, October). *The Populist Movement as seen by L. Frank Baum.* Letter to author.

Bruner, J. (1994). The importance of structure. In G. Willis & W. H. Schubert (Eds.), *The American curriculum: A documentary history.* Westport, CT: Praeger Publishers.

Carroll, L. (1897). *Alice in Wonderland: A Norton critical edition* (2nd ed.) (D. J. Gray, Ed.). New York, NY: W. W. Norton Company.

Dewey, J. (1959). My pedagogic creed. In M. E. Dworkin (Ed.), *Dewey on education: Selections.* (pp. 77–80) New York, NY: Teachers College Press.

John Dewey is probably the most read and recognized educational theorist. His focus on development, the role of doing, and child-centered, holistic education has tremendously influenced what we learn about education. Every teacher should do the work to contextualize his theories within the greater realm of critical educational theory.

Ghansah, R. K. (2015). *The radical vision of Toni Morrison.* New York, NY: New York Times Company.

Groening, M. (1990). *Lisa's substitute* [Television series episode]. In The Simpsons. Fox Television.

Groening, M. (1996). *Who shot Mr. Burns?* [Television series episode]. In The Simpsons. Fox Television.

Groening, M. (1997). *Bart goes to military school* [Television series episode]. In The Simpsons. Fox Television.

Kincheloe, J. L., & Weil, D. (Eds.). (2004). *Critical thinking and learning: An encyclopedia for parents and teachers.* Westport, CT: Greenwood Press.

Kincheloe, J. L., *Home alone and bad to the bone: the advent of a postmodern childhood.* In Steinberg, S. R., & Kincheloe, J. L. (Eds.) (2004). Kinderculture: The corporate construction of childhood. Boulder, Colo: Westview Press.

Littlefield, H. M. (1964). The wizard of oz: Parable on populism. *American Quarterly, 16*(1), 47–58. doi:10.2307/2710826.

Luthi, M. (1976). *Once upon a time: On the nature of fairy tales.* Bloomington, IN: Indiana University Press.

Moje, E., Ciechanowski, K. M., Kramer, K., Ellis, L., Carrillo, R., & Collazo, T. (2004). Working toward third space in content area literacy: An examination of everyday funds of knowledge and discourse. Reading Research Quarterly, 39, 38–70.

Morrison, T. (1970). *The bluest eye.* New York, NY: Penguin Books.

Toni Morrison is one of the mostly widely read and admired American authors of the late 20th century. Beginning her career as an instructor and editor, she went on to become a renowned force in the world of literature. Having written fiction, plays, political essays, children's literature, and opera, her creativity has few limits. Her reach and influence has extended from politics to film to rap music. Known for turning the enigmatic history of the African-American people into compelling and haunting stories, her writing has shaped and inspired people's lives.

With her novels, Morrison has established a place for herself among the classic authors whom she admired and honored with her earlier work. She has already left a very visible footprint on American culture. Her political writing is also far-reaching and influential. While she first worked to shape and to nurture the work of others as a teacher and editor, she has become a muse to other important artists. The rap artist and actor Mos Def was inspired to write a song with Talib Kweli for their first album together entitled "Thieves in the Night." This song borrows a passage from The Bluest Eye and, like The Bluest Eye, examines the impact of racism on American culture.

Morrison is also one of the most widely decorated and esteemed writers of this century. In addition to her Pulitzer Prize, she is one of nine women, and the only African-American woman, to be awarded the Nobel Prize for Literature. She continues her work as a writer, cultural critic, and as professor at Princeton University as the Robert F. Goheen Professor in the Council of Humanities. Among the many distinctions she holds, she is also the first black woman to be appointed a Chair at an Ivy League University.

Powell, J. (1997). *Derrida for beginners*. London: Writers and Readers.

Sleeter, C. E., & Grant, C. A. (1999). *Making choices for multicultural education*. Hoboken, NJ: John Wiley & Sons.

Wallace, I., & Wallechinsky, D. (1978). *The people's almanac*. New York, NY: Bantam.

Waters, H. F. (1990, April). Family feuds. *Newsweek, 23*, 58–64.

· 1 4 ·

POSSIBILITIES FOR A SOCIAL RECONSTRUCTION

This chapter is an exercise. An exercise I highly recommend you try at some point on your own. There is something remarkable that happens when you can imagine the possibilities for a school without the gravity of budgets, schedules and tests. And let me say this to you if no one ever has: You are entitled to have a vision. Teaching, as with any profession, is equal parts vision and execution. But, vision first. All of the theory, pedagogy, strategy and effort are meaningless without your vision. So have your vision; in fact have many. On one hand this is possibly self-indulgent; on the other I hope it speaks for itself.

The Vive Noir! Language Arts Academy Charter School

In 1969, Nathan Hare, the chair of San Francisco State's very progressive Black Studies Department, created a sample curriculum or program of black studies. Divided into two phases, the expressive and the pragmatic, the curriculum was designed to build pride, a collective destiny, and a sense of the past as a springboard for the future, while specifically preparing black students to deal with issues in contemporary society. What follows is in the spirit of Nathan Hare's curriculum (Hare, 1969, pp. 160–171).

A Letter to the Parents
The Vive Noir! Language Arts Academy High School

Welcome Parents!

Congratulations on your choice of Vive Noir! for your child and for your family. We are happy that you will be part of our family, and we look forward to the learning and work of the upcoming school year.

The name Vive Noir! comes from a poem by Mari Evans with the same title. The name means "To Live Black," to celebrate one of the many things that make us who we are and bind us as a community. The poem speaks of the poet's desire to reinsert "blackness" into all branches of American culture, from children's books to the tallest urban skyscrapers. This is an important message for all children to hear. All children deserve to know that their existence is unique, special, and amazing, not because they are the minority or because they are good enough to measure up to other cultures, but because they live in a world where the adults of their community will struggle every day to make sure their world is a place where all people are treated equally and all cultures are treated as important and vital.

Our vision is shaped by the vision of Dr. Martin Luther King Jr., who said that one day "the crooked places will be made straight" and "we all 'will be able to work together, to pray together, to struggle together.'" But it is also rooted in the belief that Marcus Garvey held and stated in the document entitled Declaration of Rights of the Negro Peoples of the World, "We demand the right of unlimited and unprejudiced education for ourselves and posterity forever." (Van DeBurg, 1997, p. 28)

Your child will be met with high and rigorous academic and intellectual expectations. She or he also will be furnished with many tools and skills with which to meet these expectations. And, most important, there will always be a community of dedicated teachers, administrators, and family members that is dedicated to students' growth by supporting them every step of the way.

Thanks again for making us your choice.

Sincerely,
The Vive Noir! Family

Mission and Goals

The Vive Noir! Language Arts Academy High School was established to develop the skills and abilities of all children with a natural aptitude for language and language arts. We seek to exploit these skills and interests to turn them into cultural currency that the children will take with them into higher education and throughout life. The academy is a language-immersion school that focuses on the development of language skills: reading, writing, and verbal, in both the child's native language and then in another language of his or her choice.

Beyond this, it is our goal to inspire and challenge children to think about language and how it shapes our culture and identities. The children will be posed questions about how language positions them and others in society and how it becomes a weapon of our cultural wars.

And, beyond this, the children will be expected to create and shape a position about the place they occupy in the world. Children will be expected to examine their role in the very political process of education and to decide how they plan to expand on their role to, as bell hooks (1994) says, "live more fully in the world" (p. 20).

There will be strong academic expectations of the children who attend the Vive Noir! Academy. Because it is a charter school, the children are expected to meet Chicago academic standards as well as the academy's own very specific and stringent standards. In order to accomplish all of the very ambitious goals that Vive Noir! sets forth for our students, children will be put on a very structured path so that they are not set up to fail, and so that they have all of the skills and tools necessary to embark on the further investigation of the curriculum that is expected of them in the later years of high school.

The Vive Noir! Language Arts Academy High School is a grades 9–12 secondary school situated on the South Side of Chicago. While the school seeks to serve that community in which it is located, all children are invited to become part of our learning community. We wish to stress the belief that, while the mission and philosophy of the school is rooted in the desire to empower black children, we seek to accomplish this through the empowerment of all children. This can be done by giving children the opportunity to examine the particular and, of course, very complex role they play in society because of their visual appearance, their social status, and their economic status. All children, depending on the context of the situation they find themselves in, must make choices to reject subscribed roles as oppressor or oppressed. This truth is what is at the heart of our mission. The way we seek to make this truth evident is through the education and empowerment of the children we teach to make the right choices.

The school has four departments and operates on a block schedule. The academic departments are structured so that departments can work together to plan interdisciplinary outlines for their classes. The departments are Math/Science, History/Language, Language Arts/Writing, and Humanities. Two days of each month are devoted to interdisciplinary seminar/workshops that all children attend, and at some point, all children are expected to take part in creating and facilitating. Teachers are also expected to create Field Learning Experiences for their students, which mean taking children out of the classroom and into other learning environments. Children are also expected to complete a career portfolio that reflects their four years of growth as a student at the academy as a graduation requirement. It is also required that all seniors take up an independent learning project with a teacher at the school or through working with an approved leader or educator in the community. This project must include a service learning component and meet the "Each One Teach One" tutoring requirement. Time is dedicated throughout a senior's school year to meet these requirements.

Admission to the school is also a rigorous process. Eligibility is determined by a group of factors. Candidates must take a language aptitude exam. They must also supply written work from their previous educational experiences, and grades are evaluated and considered. There must be three letters of recommendation. After candidates are screened through this process, children and their families are invited for an interview. It is encouraged but not mandatory that children have some background in another language.

The Departments and Classes
Science and Math

Our STEM classes are grounded in the ideas of Omiunota N. Ukpokodu and has as its primary focus the goal of undoing the "crisis in mathematics learning among urban and low-income students is caused by school policies, curricula, and teaching practices that do not engage those students." The STEM program at Vive Noir! Is designed around the pillars of inquiry, mastery and "that mathematics presents a great opportunity to teach and help students learn about issues of social, political, and economic justice, especially as an analytical tool for examining and understanding community and societal issues and inequities in an unjust world." This will include approaches such as arts integration; using data and scientific method to identify and solve problems in our community using technology and hands on learning experience.

All students of Vive Noir! are expected to meet a three-year math and a three-year science requirement. The classes are aligned with the goals and design of the Chicago public schools but are tailored to reflect the learning environment of the academy. These classes are taught in tandem, and where possible, the school makes a commitment to providing mutual planning time for the math and science teachers so their classes can be cotaught.

Each year, the science class will complement the math class to invite this kind of collaboration. In addition to this, there will be themes presented in the math and science classes that the learners will be expected to take up in their other classes as well. Students are encouraged to make this exploration formal so that the work can contribute to their senior-year independent learning projects. So for instance, freshman year, when the students take Earth Science and Algebra, a possible theme would be the history of ancient Egypt, the building of the pyramids, and investigation into the work of Imotep, the Father of Algebra. This work could be further developed in their history class with an investigation into how history itself is created, and how it is that we come to develop the perceptions and ideas that we have about such seemingly static things as math and science in the first place.

Teachers will be expected to develop these learning opportunities throughout the summer and the school year. Planning time will be dedicated to the teachers for this explicit purpose. In addition to this, since presenting knowledge in this fashion will place a different kind of work "burden" on the teacher, all teachers are encouraged and expected to explore and follow up on their own professional-development opportunities so they can, in effect, keep up.

The first-year students will take Earth Science and Algebra. The second-year students will take Biology and Geometry. A possible theme for these classes is "Exploring the Visual" in math and science. These ideas can be further developed in their humanities and language-arts classes, where they will be already exploring these questions. Students can do origami in geometry class or explore the work of Leonardo da Vinci and others who did work in anatomy and figures. Again, students will be expected to explore the political implications of what they have learned as well.

Junior-year students will take Chemistry and Modern Mathematics. In these courses, they will explore the contemporary implications and possibilities for math and science. Through investigation into books such as Chaos by James Glieck and For All Practical Purposes (a project directed by Solomon Garfunkel), both books that study very contemporary applications of math and science, they will be encouraged to explore the ways that math and science give us to order our own worlds and the information that we process every day.

These interdisciplinary themes will be further developed in the learning workshops/seminars that will take place during the year.

There are no senior-year math or science requirements; however, it is expected that there is a math and science component to students' final project.

Language and History

The Vive Noir! Academy is unique in that it borrows from the language-immersion model and offers its history program and classes in the elected language of the child. Students can choose from among Spanish, French, Chinese, and Swahili. The first year, the child's class will be an intensive introductory course in the child's elected language that focuses on world civilization.

The second year, the child will begin an interrogation into American contemporary culture as well as the culture/cultures that speak their chosen language.

The third year will be a more intensive look into the culture of their chosen language, especially through reading the great works of their written history. This class will begin to look at ancient history, taking up where their freshman year left off, and it will end with a specific point in the history of the culture of their chosen language.

The fourth year will return to contemporary culture and a contemporary world-history class, and at this point the students will be expected to situate the country they have studied into the greater framework of the world.

There will be many themes the students will be expected to take up and explore. These themes also will be developed in their language-arts classes as well as in their humanities classes.

It will be especially important for students to question the very strong issues surrounding language itself. For instance, why is it seen as an asset for some people to be fluent in a language, while for others it is not? Why is it that some students go to school to learn Spanish (or another language), while others go to school to unlearn it? How is language a tool of oppression? What can history tell us about this? How is language a tool of freedom? What does history tell us about this? What can we learn by looking at the diaspora of language and how that shapes cultures? What about the issue of "Black" English? How does one group's way of expression become incorrect or nonstandard, while another's is not?

Beyond this, the students will be expected to describe and explain how their grasp of a second language will be an asset to their "more fully developed life" in the future. The end goal is for the student to be a person who thinks both locally and globally and in two languages.

Language Arts and Writing

The Language Arts Program will be very demanding and will realize several goals. In brief, these goals are as follows:

1. Read with understanding and fluency.
2. Understand explicit and implicit meaning in literature representing individual, community, national, world, and historical perspectives.
3. Write to communicate for a variety of purposes.
4. Listen and speak effectively in a variety of situations.
5. Use the language arts for inquiry and research to acquire, organize, analyze, evaluate, and communicate information (p. 5).

The program will seek to accomplish these goals as well as goals that are specific to the academy, including interdisciplinary learning opportunities. As much as possible, the classes are aligned to complement the other classes in different departments to maximize on thematic learning projects.

The first year, the students will take a fundamentals class that will also double as a reading-strategies course so that students have as many tools at their disposal as possible and are able to accomplish all five learning goals. This class will introduce and establish the idea of genre and, through working with the language classes, will investigate why certain genres are particular to certain cultures. The students will read one American "classic" in this class, as a class, as well as one on their own. To investigate this book, they will team up with another student, most likely a senior who has already read the book.

In the second year, we will begin to deconstruct the notion of genre, and through working, again, with the language/history classes, we will begin to explore why fiction may be an appropriate way to express some things but not other things. Thematic projects can be built out of looking at slave narratives or other writings that firmly establish a perspective of history that may be in conflict with other perspectives we may encounter. A large part of this class will be to deconstruct the "canon" and look at how the canon was established. The students will read Zora Neal Hurston's Their Eyes Were Watching God, Alice Walker's The Color Purple, and Toni Morrison's The Bluest Eye. Students will be expected to read these books as classics, exploring the qualities that make them part of the "canon," and then against the notion that they are classics, exploring how, as Davis, Sumara and Luce-Kaplar (2000) say, Morrison "has worked to unravel the tyranny of language by using it in new ways" (p. 221). At the end of this, the students will be expected to justify why these books are American "classics" because they both embrace and confront tradition. They must come to their conclusion through a rethought definition of America and American classics.

A possible theme for interdisciplinary study will be to explore the visual aspects of these books, as students will be doing in science and math. Another possibility is to explore the "slang" and "dialects" that are used in these books in conjunction with similar variations in their chosen language of study.

Because we are a language-arts school, we will pay special attention to literacy and the multiple literacies that our students bring to our classrooms. All literacies will be treated as assets, not deficits. In order to accomplish this goal, we will create a special literacy center that is designed to serve all of our students and teachers.

Our students will come to our classroom with a range of mechanical literacy skills. One task of the Literacy Center will be to provide "Reading Recovery" skills where necessary and to provide teachers with the necessary resources and methods coaching so that they will be able to give their students the mechanical skills they need to meaningfully navigate a secondary learning program, to succeed in the multiple ways they will be assessed throughout their high-school years, and to go on to be successful college students and life-long learners. These mechanical skills will help our students grow into our larger definition of literacy.

The Literacy Coordinators will, by making the resources of the Literacy Center available to all members of the learning community, work to foster literacy across the curriculum and all areas of student learning. In addition, the Literacy Coordinators will work with teachers, students, and parents to support successful outcomes with both standardized and performance-based assessment systems that will be utilized within the schools.

The Literacy Coordinators will be a central component to all professional-development programs by providing the following services:

- Building a School Media and Resource Library and a Campus Literacy Center.
- Helping teachers to select and create curricular materials. Supporting students with their work.
- Working with area elementary schools, parents, and community members to do the work of capitalizing upon skills that the students will already bring to the learning environment.

The Literacy Center will be available to students and their families. In addition, the Literacy Coordinators will work with existing community organizations and members to support and nurture a culture of literacy outside of our school walls.

We believe the Literacy Center will contribute to an overall program of student success at the Vive Noir! Academy. This success will be made manifest in the day-to-day areas of instruction because teachers and students will have additional support, and this support will be customized to the learning styles of our students and to the unique missions of the schools.

Since we will have students that represent multiple languages and literacies, it is also our hope that the Literacy Center will create concrete opportunities for the students to acquire language and language skills from one another. We believe that this will contribute to a larger culture of community and shared learning and give us an opportunity to build bridges for our students where there are typically walls. Among the many outcomes we hope to see as a result of building the Literacy Center, we hope to see our students master their own languages, the languages of power, and the languages of their neighboring communities as well. We are confident that these skills and experiences will support their endeavors as college students and contributing community members, too.

As a teaching and learning community, we feel that traditional approaches to teaching and assessing literacy in schools have failed our students. We suggest a new definition of literacy that departs from the mechanics of decoding to encompass these ideas:

- Literacy must be contextualized within the social/political dynamics of the students' lives.

- Literacy must go beyond decoding letters and mechanical skills.
- Literacy is not neutral and not a basic skill. Literacy includes a relationship "in which learners can mediate the struggle for emancipation, democracy, social justice, and transformative practices."
- Cultural proficiency and cultural literacy are tools for students to "embrace and understand aspects of dominant culture that will provide a basis for transformation of wider social order."
- "It is important to master the dominant language for accessing the wider world, but not at the expense of individual identities."
- Children must not be silenced. Literacy must not be taught in a "banking system" (mechanical, direct instruction) but rather in a "problem-posing" (child-centered, inquiry-based) system so that teacher and student work together to build meaning.
- Literacy is the most crucial component in a student's success or failure in school. The literacy program will empower students (Garcia & Valenzuela, 2004, pp. 278–280).

Humanities

The Humanities Department will have the very crucial task of bringing the work of the other departments together so that the students are learning in a comprehensive, cohesive way. This means the role of the Humanities Department will be primarily to reinforce the learning that takes place in the other classes and to build on the interdisciplinary themes that are developed throughout the year. The curriculum of the Humanities Department will be a learning curriculum that changes according to the climate of the school as well as the strengths and needs of the students. The humanities teacher will function as a sort of advisor and will most likely be the teacher with whom the senior students complete their final projects.

The Vive Noir! Language Arts Academy Charter School has as its most important goal the development and empowerment of the whole child. By focusing on what are inherent gifts, the school seeks to develop the whole child with a life-long love for learning that has been nurtured and encouraged throughout the child's educational experience with us. In addition to this, the child will leave with two very important skills: the ability to speak another language and the ability to look at his or her world critically while feeling ready and able to make a difference in it.

References

Davis, B., Sumara, D., & Luce-Kapler, R. (2000). Engaging minds. Mahwah, NJ: Lawrence Erlbaum Associates.

Garcia, H. S., & Valenzuela, T. (2004). Gaining access to critical literacy: Rethinking the role of reading programs. In J. L. Kincheloe & D. Weil (Eds.), *Critical thinking and learning: An encyclopedia for parents and teachers* (pp. 278–280). Westport, CT: Greenwood Press.

Gleick, J. (1988). *Chaos: Making a new science.* New York, NY: Penguin.

Hare, N. (1969). Questions and answers about black students. In W. L. Van DeBurg (Ed.), *Modern black nationalism: From Marcus Garvey to Louis Farrakhan* (pp. 160–71). New York, NY: New York University Press.

Van DeBurg, W. L. (Ed.). (1997). *Modern black nationalism: From Marcus Garvey to Louis Farrakhan.* New York, NY: New York University Press.

· 1 5 ·

EVERY SCHOOL, EVERY SUBJECT—
STEM AND CLASSROOM CULTURE

The relationship between STEM and social justice education possibly best demonstrates exactly why there is a need for a social reconstructionist approach to education. Women and people of color are staggeringly underrepresented in STEM fields now and have been historically. http://www.usnews.com/news/stem-solutions/articles/2014/02/06/minorities-women-still-underrepresented-in-stem-fields-study-finds

It is generally accepted that disparities in math and science performance are the result of vast disparities in educational quality in the U.S. Research shows that schools with large numbers of racial and ethnic minorities, low-income students, and English language learners (ELL) are systematically under resourced compared with schools serving middle and upper class and White students. They have fewer well-trained teachers, fewer advanced courses, and less access to academic basics—from pencils and paper to computers and calculators. It all adds up to students from historically marginalized groups having significantly fewer "opportunities to learn" than their more advantaged peers. However, when students from nonmainstream backgrounds receive equitable learning opportunities, they are capable of attaining science outcomes comparable to their mainstream peers. The same is true for mathematics and, presumably, for other STEM subjects, as well.

So, possibly the dots between schools and the bigger world are easier to connect when it comes to STEM education, and yet, many STEM teachers believe that social justice education and STEM are parallel to one another. So, let's think about the ways that these two worlds can intersect.

The goal of representation in schools and outside of schools in crucial and absolutely a great place to start, but the intersection must go way beyond representation. Identifying and sharing examples of underrepresented groups in STEM fields should be done often and consistently, but we also need to examine our thinking about how scientific and mathematical thinking is constructed and what knowledge is legitimized over other knowledge.

We need to expand the linear constructs of STEM thinking and be responsive to our students' imaginations and curiosities. We need to think beyond the neutrality and objectivity of the STEM subjects and make more room for questioning, challenging, and resisting in our STEM curriculum.

We need to value and leverage our students' funds of knowledge in our STEM classrooms. Ukpokodu (2011) offers the example of students that missed a word problem concerning the use of a weekly bus pass instead of a daily bus pass:

> Unfortunately, the students failed this item because they had contextualized their thinking within the context of their lived experiences as they thought and applied the multiple uses for the pass—working seven days a week (not just five days), going to two or more jobs, for rides to visit relatives, social events, church, and allowing relatives or friends to use it.

Most importantly, we need to situate our STEM curriculum in the lives of our students and make STEM a vehicle for problem solving and activism for our classrooms. Learning units like the Environmental Justice Movement created by the Congressional Black Caucus, that explore environmental injustices, empowering students to not only identify problems in their communities but also to solve these problems working together to become agents of change as well. Making space in the curriculum for students to use STEM as a way to authentically engage their world will create better outcomes in both our schools and in the STEM vocational and professional fields as well.

Management and SRC

Ideas and best practice about classroom management, like most concerns in schools, will change and evolve through years and experiences. Management is incredibly particular to the individual teacher and so, as with describing strategies for culturally relevant instruction and curriculum, it would be a mistake to say to any teacher: This is how you do it. What I am sharing here are the things I can share that are theoretically sound but also road tested.

The trend in most teacher preparation programs seems to be focus on pedagogy and classroom culture but to avoid direct discussion about management and discipline (teach for America articles). I know this was the case for me and it is the number one concern that first year teachers bring to me when I check in with them. They just didn't feel ready.

I am going to be honest. Brutally honest. It is not uncommon for new teachers to find themselves, depending on where they have been hired or placed, to experience complete culture shock. This isn't because one culture is inherently better, smarter, or calmer, or whatever; it is because things are different. The trouble starts when stressed out, overwhelmed, underprepared teachers begin to build resistance, intolerance as a way to cope with what they are experiencing instead of building strategies, and a solid, reflective practice. Having said this, the thing that we do wrong as the teachers of teacher is perpetuate the silly idea that if there are problems in a class, no matter what is the teacher's fault. If the leadership in the school or training program is telling this teacher that they just need to have higher expectations and build relationships, while ducking the class space and silently giving thanks it isn't their problem, then the leadership is failing. And, while high expectations and building relationships are pretty critical components of an excellent, socially just classroom, they are a part of an entire system in which the confidence of the teacher, in herself and in her entire support system also matter.

And, I will say what a lot of others won't. Some kids are jerks. Some parents are jerks. You may have entire classes that you just don't like. You will love them. You will absolutely teach them. But you don't have to like them. And that's OK. The idea that a teacher is somehow failing if they are not walking on sunshine every day of their working lives is ridiculous, unfair and a set up for failure. Some days the dragon wins.

But, you know what else? Don't confuse work with vacation. It is work. It is supposed to be hard. It is work. Yes, without question, teachers should and must stay passionate and enthusiastic about what we do. And, we will; we do. But this doesn't mean that we don't have bad days. And I will tell you another thing: Any teacher that says that haven't had bad days, or a certain student that made them miserable, and treats you as though you are weak or a sissy because you are struggling is also a jerk. And a liar. Every teacher has struggled with management. Every teacher has had a student that hurt them personally and fought back emotion in order to maintain order. It happens. And if a teacher is unprepared, unfamiliar, and overwhelmed, it can happen a lot.

The good news is that we can do this. We are teachers. This is what we do. Depending on the context, there are lots of ways to think about and talk about classroom management. Dig in and find what works; the most effective strategies will be the things you can do authentically and with confidence. Be yourself, but be the strongest version of yourself.

And here is more good news: Every once in a while you get a class that just clicks beautifully. The students get along; there may be some charmers or secret favorites; there is a chemistry and things just work. There is a magic. This is the class where you will be at your optimal best. You will be able to take some risks and you will get to really push your practice and your passion. Every class is not this class, but the stronger you get the more it seems like every class comes pretty close.

At the end of all of this is the powerful thing that while it isn't true that a lousy class is only your fault, it does pretty much come down to us. This is powerful, not crushing, because it means that there are endless things we can do to make our classrooms high functioning, brilliant and well-oiled machines that our students don't hate as much as other classes, or maybe even love.

I have a few staples I share with my students. The first is my favorite because it makes me laugh. I have a friend who grew up in a city where there were few swimming pools, so, like a lot of kids who grew up in big cities, he never learned how to swim. When he got older he joined a nice gym with an Olympic size swimming pool, and he decided he was finally going to learn. He is an intelligent and take charge kind of guy, so the first thing he did was went to the book store and bought a book about swimming.

I usually stop there because (some of) the students are already laughing along with me and my tricky point has been made: You can't learn to swim without getting in the pool. This is the sometimes tough thing about managing and facilitating a learning environment: You have to be patient and give experience time to develop. A lot of this really comes with experience and just the time to try things out and develop confidence in your own presence and authority. Experience brings the repetition of certain things so by the 70th time something has happened, it no longer floors you and your response is just reflex. Experience also brings the realization that you actually don't have to put up with that and that your students really don't have to go to the bathroom, and more importantly, that nothing is going to disrupt the flow in your classroom, that is your students at work and learning. So, if you're a new teacher, give experience some time and have trust in yourself and the process. I can say, too, that what inexperienced teachers lack in field hours, they make up for in energy and enthusiasm. Embrace where you're at.

Here are the truths I have found while swimming my own course.

1. The first and most important thing I would tell any teacher, new or veteran, is that the best defense is a good offense. It is the fundamental truth of teaching. An exciting, engaging, well-planned, and structured classroom is going to solve 99% of your problems and make your world brighter and more enjoyable. Teachers forget somehow that kids don't like school. For the most part, kids and school are sworn enemies. If your classroom is absorbing enough, your students might actually forget they're in school. This is a tall order, without doubt, and requires a level of planning that rivals a solar space mission. But, it is worth it and I have seen glorious example after glorious example of classrooms and students completely turned around when the instruction comes together.

This involves all reaches of your instruction. Find examples of classrooms with creative and exciting setups and use of space. Make use of all five senses: When I taught high school, even in the deepest winter, I opened the windows and sprayed my room while one of my students picked up the room and straightened the seats. I played music and put something in students' hands—a post-it note to record the bell ringer response or a picture from a magazine that they would use as a writing prompt. The purpose is to interrupt whatever they're focused on and bring their focus to our class.

Once you have their attention you need to keep it. This, too, comes down to planning. You have to know your content. Any kid worth her salt will know immediately and exploit any hint that you don't know the content you are teaching. You have to know your content back and forth and as much as possible, you better have some passion for that content too.

You have to know your pedagogy and have to have on hand more than a few ways to deliver your content. Get online: For any one thing you are teaching, the global teachers' lounge will show you thirty different ways to teach that lesson. Goals and objectives should be clear and relevant. One of the biggest teaching epiphanies I've had was simple: write the goals, guiding questions and plan somewhere for the students to see so the class has structure and purpose.

You have to know your students; build on their own life (Eggen & Kauchak, 1997, p. 54) experiences and have high expectations of what each student is capable of learning and producing. Learn what it is that each student is really interested in and curious about and then exploit that energy in service of your own class.

You may have noticed that I haven't yet mentioned anything particularly related to social reconstructionism, or even culture, at all. I will make this point several times throughout this book: An outstanding, brilliant, inspired classroom is, considered alone, an act of interruption. This is true for any classroom, and if we are thinking as social reconstructionists, then it is particularly true of underserved classrooms. Outstanding classrooms make this change possible and creating outstanding learning opportunities to correct the debt owed to underserved children is an act of radical defiance.

2. Plan your routines and procedures and work your plan. There are several resources to help with this part of facilitating your classroom. Start with Wong and Wong The First Days of School and Jones, Jones & Jones Tools for Teaching. Get on Amazon and read the reviews so you can figure out which resources will work best for you. Your colleagues are your real life resource. Observe classrooms and adopt and adapt the routines that work.

3. Yes, check your bias but also get to know your students in their neighborhoods and communities. Not just where the interesting restaurants that only the true foodies in your city know about, but the community your kids live their lives in. Where do your students go to see the doctor? Where do they get their shoes? Know their routes. Take the bus they take home every day. Research shows that one thing that exemplary teachers of African-American children share is that they believe they are a part of the community (Ladson-Billings, 2000, p. 479).

Learn about how your students interact with their parents and families. This is how you become culturally responsive and proficient. How do their moms talk with them? Research and experience shows us that parenting styles can differ largely from culture to culture. Research shows us that African-American moms describe themselves as "no nonsense," less permissive, and more in control than their European counterparts. (Challenges) But there is also evidence of a high degree of warmth and effective authoritative parenting. In our classrooms this translates to what we are now calling warm demandingness. Warm demandingness may appear harsh to the uniformed observer, but in fact is shown to be incredibly effective with children in high poverty schools where students are accustomed to firm, no nonsense management that comes from a place of unconditional love and protectiveness. Elizabeth Bondy and Dorene

D. Ross (2001) describe this approach in their article titled The Teacher as Warm Demander. They tell us that,

> Although classroom teachers have little control over many factors that affect student engagement, they do have the means to create a supportive climate that fosters engagement among high-poverty students. Warm demanders do so by approaching their students with unconditional positive regard, knowing students and their cultures well, and insisting that students perform to a high standard. Students have told researchers that they want teachers who communicate that they are "important enough to be pushed, disciplined, taught, and respected." (Wilson & Corbett, 2001, p. 88)
> Such is the stance of the warm demander.

Find your own warm demandingness and make it your own.

Does their faith and religious or spiritual practice play a large role in their day-to-day lives? If so, visit their place of worship and learn more about how their faith can be a tool for knowing and appreciating their family. Are you afraid in the neighborhood and around their homes? Try to do home visits. Home visits can be infinitely positive for everyone. And revealing. They can reveal things about your kids and, even more, things about yourself. Are you scanning the walls and making judgments or are you comfortable and warming up to the world your students live in everyday? And while you're at it, spend some time interacting with different kinds of people, including the folks that live in the community where you teach. This is a pretty simple idea, and yet, over my years as a teacher the majority of the teachers I taught or worked with did not spend additional time in the communities they worked in. Let's say you are a new teacher and also a white person who really hasn't spent time with any people of color before. There is a pretty good chance your students have interacted with other white people in their lives. So, remember that: You aren't the first or only white person they have ever dealt with. However, if you have not spent time with any people of color it will be pretty obvious and a major disadvantage. As well it should be. If you are uncomfortable your body language will betray you. You owe it to yourself and your students to get comfortable and familiar with your community, which will be your second home, after all. Here is the best thing: If your school's neighborhood is dangerous, there is a way to learn and explore so that you won't be conspicuous, intrusive or vulnerable. Recruit a parent to take all of the teachers on a walking tour; make a point to do your grocery shopping there on before heading home; offer to take a student and their little siblings to the playground one day and give their mom a break. Now you'll have a second home where you feel comfortable and a sense of belonging, not out of place and apprehensive.

4. I had a friend who, when I first started teaching, would remind me that kids don't sh**. Of course, like a good teacher I pushed back at this idea, but she may have been on to something. Children, literally, are developing the capacity for understanding and anticipating the consequences of their actions (Eggen & Kauchak, 1997, p. 476). Remember your role in the process. Do not, under any circumstances, argue with your students or escalate incidents and issues (p. 476). This comes with experience, but it can be established from the onset. Do not get locked into patterns of interaction with students, and if you start to see a pattern like that developing, interrupt it with a positive, more productive exchange. Always allow for new ways of relating to a student to come about. Be clear to yourself about your own goal. If your goal is to assert your authority and win an argument, you won't. Your goal should always be to move your class and your individual students forward to learn as much as possible in that moment. Ask a colleague that you trust to spend some time in your classroom as a participant. Something as simple as this can shift energy, interrupt any unhelpful patterns you might be unknowingly locked in, and create potential for new approaches, perspectives and ways for your relationships to grow.

5. Know the difference between behavior and attitude. Manage your expectations around both. Identify which behaviors you want to promote or decrease in your classroom, and remember that you can get a student to change their behavior but a change in attitude may happen later or never at all. In all ways, make your classroom a place that encourages and allows for constructive behaviors (p. 216). As much as possible, focus on the behaviors you want to see and praise the students for working hard and contributing to the community.

Raise the bar. This is an idea that was hard to get my mind around and even now, I have to think about this and be very intentional and thoughtful about how to raise the bar for students when training and intuition says to punish. Here is one for instance: if you have a student who is constantly throwing trash on the floor, rather than punish him with consequences that don't connect to the problem, put this child in charge of setting up a bulletin board. Sharing responsibility for the classroom environment raises the bar and a student who feels pride and ownership of his classroom will not want to destroy it. I'm sure that, even for the most joyful or seasoned teacher, a classroom without punishment seems ridiculous and impractical at best. But, just imagine this for the sake of imagining it. In an ideal world, with all of the necessary time and support, we could raise the bar even higher. For any undesirable action we could, instead of punishing the student tit for tat, identify one or even more related actions that contribute to the community and then take the time to guide and work with the student to work through and learn from the experience. Impossible? Maybe, but, consider it and then next time you are dealing with something in your own, real life, classroom, raise the bar.

This absolutely matters in the culturally responsive, interruptive classroom. In the larger context of school to prison pipelines and achievement gaps, raising the bar, and moving away from culture of punishment for our students is equally disruptive and radical.

6. And, lastly, there is this. There are a (hopefully small) few of us who have heard or told stories of teaching in urban, low-poverty schools being nothing short of riot control and clinging to life, hoping to make it to the end of the year so you can fun fast and far from teaching and schools forever.

There are the stories of the earnest, hopeful, and well-meaning young people who go into classrooms, possibly as part of an alternative teacher training program, only to come out beaten, broken rejected, and incredulous. Don't be that guy. Doctors train for about a decade before becoming officially ready to practice on their patients. Teaching is a complex, arduous professional practice as well, so why would we believe a teacher can be practice successfully after five weeks? For students to lose months and years of instructional time because their teachers are unprepared, is not only tragic for the teachers, it is educational malpractice, and it is an overt act of institutional oppression and violence. So, don't be that guy.

In the universe of socially just and reconstructionist education there are a things that teaching is not:

- Teaching is not something to be tried out on the way to finding out what you really want to do or want become.
- Teaching is not an altruistic box to be checked on the way to doing the work that you really want to do.
- Teaching is not easy, it is not babysitting and it is not for those who can't do what it is they really should be doing or those who can't do anything else.

Have some respect.

You can and should interview and investigate any school you are considering. Find the exemplary schools and if you come across a school that is a place where well-meaning young people go to become bitter and disillusioned, then don't take that job. The very idea of putting the teachers who are newly emerging and establishing their own practice with students to whom we owe the biggest debt is reprehensible and I warmly demand that you consider taking a different path. To be clear: I am not in any way claiming that new teachers, inexperienced teachers, or alternatively certified teachers can't and shouldn't teach. In fact, I stand by the thinking that some of the very best teachers are those that are just beginning and willing to try everything and anything, willing to put themselves out there and uplifting their school with the energy to match.

If you are that guy and you are still reading then your job is to read, work, learn, and do as much as you can to care for yourself so you can stay afloat and do as much as you can for your students. In any context, the job of the new teacher is to inundate each working moment with resources and support. Find out which teachers are the most successful and buy them coffee. Align yourself with them and avail yourself of their support and knowledge. Lean on your administration, your school community, your parents but go to them with a clear plan and sense of how they can support you and your classroom, not just a desperate flail.

Equally as important is that you pace yourself and practice self-care so you can always renew your practice and you can always work for transformation.

References

Bondy, E., & Ross, D. D. (2001). *The teacher as warm demander Wilson & Corbett* (p. 88).

Eggen, P., & Kauchak, D. (1997). *Educational psychology.* Upper Saddle River, NJ: Prentice Hall.

Ladson-Billings, G. (2000). Teaching in dangerous times. *Re-Thinking Schools, 14*(4). 242–250.

Ukpokodu, O. N. (2011, Spring). How do I reach mathematics in a culturally responsive way? Multicultural Education. 19(3). 47–56

Wilson, B. L., & Corbett, H. D. (2001). *Listening to urban kids: School reform and the teachers they want.* Albany, NY: State University of New York Press.

· 1 6 ·

LESSON PLAN: HOW DO WE GET FROM HERE TO THERE?

Preschool will do thematic units that take between two weeks and a month to complete. Under the canopy of these interdisciplinary thematic units, the children will learn all subjects and practice all of the skills necessary to move on to kindergarten. This unit will be a transportation unit called "How do we get from here to there?"

Unfortunately, many school resources will present transportation in a way that confuses children and gives them misinformation. Often, these resources present developing nations or any place that is not the U.S. as primitive and not technically advanced. African-American children are often surprised to learn that people in African countries drive cars or fly in airplanes.

The truth is that most nations, like the U.S., are tremendously complex, consisting of rural and urban areas, as well as varied geographic regions. The way people "go" depends on the geography of where they live. Of course, the method of transportation also will be influenced by economic resources. These are things that we will explore in this unit.

Still, no matter which way they choose to "go," all people are joined by the fact that they have to go from here to there every day of their lives. Taking this look at transportation will give the children an opportunity to learn about the daily lives of people from all over the world, while thinking about how transportation connects us all as human beings both literally and metaphorically.

Teachers often ask how they can incorporate the goals of social justice and cross-cultural multiculturalism into their lessons. Most often, cross-cultural multiculturalism and social justice are treated as separate and relegated to small corners of our classrooms. One of the goals of this unit is to demonstrate that we cannot only incorporate our goals into units, but social justice and cross-cultural, responsible, critical, global multiculturalism can be the foundation of everything we teach.

Theme

Transportation: "How do we get from here to there?"

Learning Connections

Math: Counting wheels, classification

Social Studies: Reading maps, learning about migration, learning about the state of the world and how gasoline and oil are resources people fight over, learning about the daily lives of people who live in different places, learning about how people make choices regarding their methods of transportation, learning about how everyone in the world relies on some method of transportation, learning about why people take trips to other places. Class will explore how they get to school every day. How do our journeys differ from other students in the world?

Science: Learning about how different methods of transportation affect the environment; learning that the effects of transportation are not always positive; learning about the benefits of public transportation, especially in big cities; learning about how different methods of transportation work.

Reading/Language Arts: Library will have all different types of transportation books. Children will practice transportation sight words: bus, car, bike, etc. Children will tell their own stories about their experiences traveling. Children will read books that reflect the daily lives of people in other countries and demonstrate that all countries have access to transportation and that choices made are influenced by economic resources and geographic conditions. Class will explore how having access to transportation makes our lives easier.

Art: Children will draw pictures of themselves traveling with someone they care about or traveling to see someone they care about along with the method of transportation they used to get there.

Large Motor/Small Motor: Children will ride bikes, use other play toys with wheels, play with toy vehicles in sand table, and play with toy vehicles on rugs.

Assessment
By the end of the unit, children should be able to identify different vehicles and tell what they are for and where they are used. They will be able to tell a story about an experience they had traveling on a vehicle. They will be able to identify a group of transportation sight words and use them in context.

Culminating Activity
A trip around the preschool world: Children will be issued bus passes and passports and will be able to take a trip around the world in the preschool classroom. Children will choose methods of transportation based on geographic conditions of where they are traveling.

Today's Lesson
Learning objectives.

- Children will identify and label different vehicles.
- Children will classify different types of vehicles according to where they are used.
- Children will predict which vehicle individuals will choose as their method of transportation.
- Children will compare and contrast different methods of transportation.
- Children will demonstrate how transportation connects individuals.
- Children will practice fine motor skills by placing vehicles on a landscape board.
- Children will be introduced to images of people from different countries in a way that will counter stereotypes.

Activities.

- Teacher will introduce lesson by reading "The Big Trip" to children as a whole group. Discussion will follow.
- Teacher will show children different landscapes and different vehicles.
- Teacher will prompt children with a situation for each vehicle.
- Children will decide as a class where each vehicle belongs; an individual child will place it on landscape board.

The lesson will close with a discussion about taking trips with friends like the characters from the story did.

· 1 7 ·

LESSON PLANS: POETRY LESSON: HOW TO WRITE THE GREAT AFRICAN-AMERICAN NOVEL

Reading for Information

According to Alfred W. Tatum (2005), author of Teaching Reading to Black Adolescent Males, in order for students to engage the reading material in the classroom, the material must recognize and reflect the turmoil that is present in the lives of adolescent young men of color. Beyond this, effective instruction must do the following:

- Provide opportunities for students to be visible, for their experiences to be validated, and for their voices to be heard.
- Reading material must reflect, rather than alienate, the students' lives and experiences and must have relatable male characters.
- High-interest text should be used as an "entry point" for students. It should scaffold learning and literacy with more difficult texts.
- Teachers must know students' lives and experiences and therefore use texts to encourage and connect students to read in order to learn more about themselves and the world.
- Teachers must not be afraid to engage students in discussions about their place in the world and within the community. These questions and discussions are crucial to a successful literacy program.

- Students should be placed in groups in order to facilitate small-group activities, responsibilities, and discussion.
- Multiple literacies must be recognized and validated. Teachers should use students' prior knowledge and literacy to scaffold learning and transform this knowledge into translatable skills such as essay writing and test taking.

The first lesson is based on the poetry of Native American poet and filmmaker Sherman Alexie (1996). Students will read and discuss Alexie's poem "How to Write the Great American Indian Novel."

After reading and discussing the poem, students will model the poem, composing their own poem called "How to Write the Great African American Novel." Afterward, students will present their poems during a poetry reading.

Objectives

- Students will expand word knowledge and be exposed to and comprehend basic poetry terms such as free verse, imagery, metaphor, extended metaphor, simile, and analogy.
- Students will interpret text for meaning and relevance. Students will use text and prior knowledge to justify an interpretation and evaluation of a text.
- Students will analyze how writers use text to express ideas and points of view.
- Students will draft, edit, and produce work for submission.

Important Vocabulary

- Analogy
- Tragic
- Half-breed
- Savage
- Visions
- Proximity
- Culture
- Metaphor
- Simile
- Image

Before Lesson
Students will do a Web Quest for Native American Indians and compile a list of 10 facts that they have discovered about their history, culture, or present-day lives.

During Lesson

Part 1.
The class will read Alexie's poem and discuss. The teacher will lead whole-class discussion by introducing prompt questions, such as:

1. What is Alexie's point of view in this poem? What technique and tone does he use to express his point of view?
2. What is Alexie's point of view toward or characterization of white people in this poem?
3. How does Alexie's experience of being an American Indian male compare with your experience of being a young, urban male of color?

After a brief class discussion, students will break into groups to have small-group discussion to answer these questions as well as two more questions that are posed by group. The whole class will resume and complete discussion, this time led by two discussion leaders.

Part 2.
Students will draft, edit, and publish their poems for presentation. Poems will be entitled "How to Write the Great African American Novel" and will model Alexie's poem. During class writing time, students will work alone or in small groups. The teacher will be available for feedback and assistance.

Part 3.
Students will read their poems in class.

Assessment
Project grades will be determined by the following:

• Participation in discussion or journal entry in response to poem.
• Final draft of poem to be completed for student's portfolio.
• Pop verbal or written quiz on vocabulary.
• Attentiveness and responsiveness to other readers during poetry reading.
• Optional small project to be completed after lesson.

Lesson Plan 4:
Reading for Information Lesson
    Using nonfiction, reality-based short writing samples, students will see that their reading and writing skills and interests are compatible with and applicable to the reading and writing of standardized tests.

Objectives
Students will:

- Make predictions about outcomes.
- Use context to identify word meaning.
- Apply prior knowledge in order to find information.
- Comprehend and synthesize abstract concepts.
- Identify main idea.
- Use metacognition to navigate standardized tests.

Important Vocabulary

- Define
- Identify
- Main idea
- Apply
- Context
- Abstract concept
- Predict

Before Lesson
Students will compile three lists:

- One list of 10 skills they have used to answer standardized-test questions correctly.
- One list of problems they have encountered with tests or reasons the tests are an unfair assessment of individual skills.
- One list of reasons to do well on tests.

Students will share their lists or put them in a journal.

During Lesson

Part 1.

The teacher will demonstrate a reading sample on the overhead. The class will read and answer questions, discussing skills used to find correct answers. Skills/vocabulary words (with definitions) will be put on word wall and posted.

- Students will do timed reading of high-interest excerpts compiled by teachers.
- Students will swap and score tests.
- Students will have five minutes to discuss with a partner how they came to correct and incorrect answers.

Part 2.

Students will be given a list of terms (important vocabulary) and in groups of three be responsible for demonstrating comprehension of each term. Demonstrations can be written, oral, acted out, or otherwise demonstrated.

Part 3.

Students will be given readings that are not "high interest." Students will work in teams to use acquired skills to answer questions. Tests will be scored. Entire class will discuss how the skills applied to new reading.

Part 4.

Students will do timed reading of new "low-interest" material and answer questions in a simulated test-taking environment.

Assessment
Students will be assessed:

- On demonstrating comprehension of important vocabulary terms.
- On applying newly acquired skills to new test.
- On contribution to group and whole-class work.

References

Alexie, S. (1996). *The summer of black widows*. New York, NY: Hanging Loose Press.

Tatum, A. W. (2005). *Teaching reading to black adolescent males: Closing the achievement gap*. Portland, ME: Stenhouse Publishers.

· 1 8 ·

A THOUGHTFUL TIMELINE

...the major thrust of a critical pedagogy should center around generating knowledge
that presents concrete possibilities for empowering people. To put it more specifically,
a critical pedagogy needs a language of possibility, one that provides the pedagogical
basis for teaching democracy while simultaneously making school more democratic.

(Giroux, 1981, p. 51)

To create an assemblage of knowledge and claim that it is the defining foundation for a critical pedagogy would actually conflict with the very principles
of critical pedagogy. The following section is not meant to be prescriptive nor
reductive, and absolutely not definitive. The reader is invited to add, subtract,
and diverge.

The timeline represents a narrow series of events that I believe make a case
for the existence of racism, classism, and sexism in this country—primarily in
schools. I have found that when faced with ignorance of (or resistance to) the
need to understand how these forces shape our worlds as educators, it helps to
have concrete, positivistic evidence that supports my position.

The glossary is also a very partial list of terms, concepts, and theories that
I have found it helpful to have some grasp of in order to navigate the sometimes choppy waters of a critical curriculum.

The annotated bibliography, also, is meant to acquaint the reader with some of the thinkers and theorists that have significantly impacted my work. This list is by no means exhaustive, and truthfully, it couldn't be. It would be impossible to credit all of those who have made meaningful and indispensable contributions to this field.

Timeline

Some may argue that the existence of institutional racism, sexism, or classism is invented at worst, or long past at best. For those who need positivistic proof that hegemonic forces do indeed shape our world and our classrooms, or that education is the primary arena for these forces to establish and maintain themselves, here are 10 incidents that offer indisputable proof. For those of you who require evidence in order to be hopeful that our schools can be the location of change, these events will show that as well.

1. The Approval of the Institution of Slavery
In the early 1600s, the first Africans are brought to America to be sold as indentured servants. By 1639, the first slave codes are entered in Virginia law books. Slave codes are the laws that regulate the buying and selling of human beings as property or real estate. It is illegal for slaves to learn to read or write, and laws are passed such as the South Carolina "Negro Act," which make it illegal for slaves to "move abroad, assemble in groups, raise food, earn money, or learn to read English." Rebellion is legally punished by death (Slavery and the Making of America, 2004a, 2004b, p. 1).

2. Emancipation Proclamation, the 15th Amendment, and the Legality of Voting
After the 15th Amendment makes it possible for African-American men to vote in 1870, Literacy Tests are required in order to establish the ability of voters to make decisions about candidates. Since it had been illegal for slaves to learn to read or write English, most freed men are unable to pass the Literacy Tests and, therefore, are unable to vote. These tests are given only to black voters.

3. *Plessy v. Ferguson*
In 1892, Homer Plessy is found guilty of refusing to leave a white railcar in Louisiana. After an appeal to the Supreme Court, the decision is upheld and Justice Henry Brown establishes the "separate but equal" precedent by

explaining that the law does not conflict with the 13th Amendment, which abolished slavery.

4. *Brown v. Board of Education*
Plessy v. Ferguson establishes that it is legal for schools to segregate based on color so long as the facilities are equal for both blacks and whites. In 1951, Oliver Brown attempts to enroll his daughter in the white public school that is seven blocks away from her house and is refused. Instead, she is supposed to walk through a rail switchyard to the black school, which is a mile away. The NAACP takes up her case, and in 1954, *Plessy v. Ferguson* is overturned for public education in a unanimous decision of the Supreme Court. It is determined that "segregation of children in public schools solely on the basis of race, even though physical facilities and other 'tangible' factors may be equal, deprive the children of the minority group of equal educational opportunities" (*Brown v. Board of Education*, PBS.org, p. 1).

5. Affirmative Action
In 1965, President Johnson renames the Compensatory Preferential Treatment Program as the Affirmative Action Program, and this sets a number of policies into motion that affect, among other things, the number of minorities that enter higher education. Affirmative action is an umbrella name now given to policies or programs that are designed to increase representation or opportunities for the minority members of society. This program continues to be controversial and largely misunderstood.

6. Title IX
In 1972, Congresswoman Patsy T. Mink writes the Title IX Educational Amendment, which makes it illegal for schools that are federally funded to spend fewer dollars in support of women's sports than they do in support of men's sports. The law goes far beyond athletics and applies to "every aspect of federally funded education programs" (Exercise My Rights, 2006, p. 1).

7. Establishment of the Texas Textbook Committee
In 1983, the Texas State Textbook Committee is established and makes decisions under strong influence from the Gablers, a family that runs the nonprofit Educational Research Analysts and believes that "publishers have conceded to the demands of feminists and minorities," that "inquiry" is a dangerous word, and that "allowing a student to come up with his own conclusions about abstract concepts creates frustration. Ideas, situations, ethics, values, anti-God Humanism—that's what the schools are teaching." The

committee must approve all the texts used in Texas public schools, and it establishes strict guidelines about what should or shouldn't be included in K–12 textbooks; in addition, they routinely ban books from acceptable book lists. In accordance with Texas law, it is determined, among other things, that the texts must prepare students to be patriotic. Because Texas "ranks fourth in national dollar expenditures on textbooks," it is virtually unprofitable for a textbook company to produce a book that does not conform to Texas approval (Thomas B. Fordham Institute, The Mad, Mad World of Textbook Adoption, 2006, p. 1).

8. Unz Initiative
In 1998, Proposition 227, or the Unz (English for the Children) Initiative, is passed in California and "successfully dismantled most bi-lingual education programs" (One Nation, 1997, p. 2). Three years later, Arizona passes a similar law. Ron Unz, a Silicon Valley millionaire and aspiring politician, used his own money to campaign for this initiative, claiming to be "pro-immigrant" and caring for children who should be united under the English language, "our common bond" (One Nation, 1997, p. 2).

9. The Little Village Lawndale Hunger Strike
After years of being promised a new high school, a group of mothers in Chicago's Little Village neighborhood stage a 19-day hunger strike from May 13 until June 2, 2001, which results in the Chicago public schools building a $68 million high school to serve the Southwest Side (Stovall, 2005, p. 1). In Chicago, which at the time had the highest murder rate of any city in the U.S., 49.8% of the public-school children are African-American and 38.0% are Latino. Only 8.8% are white, despite the fact that whites make up 41.97% of the city's population. Blacks and Latinos are concentrated in the Little Village and neighboring Lawndale communities. In the time that the Chicago public schools had promised the Little Village neighborhood a school and failed on this promise, two new schools were built in neighborhoods that serve populations of largely white students. Other staggering statistics: Young black males are nine times more likely to be murdered than their white counterparts (Dinges, 1990, p. 1). These students are less likely to graduate from high school and go on to graduate from college. Despite these dismal numbers, it took a hunger strike to get a new school built in one of the city's most dangerous, overcrowded, and underserved neighborhoods.

10. California Legal Victory for Teacher

In 2002, a Hayward, California, court rules in favor of a San Leandro High School teacher who was sued for discussing racism and homophobia in his classroom. It is determined that he does not have to seek permission from his administrators to discuss these issues in his classroom, and forcing him to do so would be in violation of his right to free speech (GLSEN, 2002, p. 1).

References

FairTest: The National Center for Fair & Open Testing. (2004). *How standardized testing damages education.* Retrieved February 18, 2004 from http://www.fairtest.org/facts/howharm.htm

GLSEN. (2002). *California's legal victory protects teachers.* Retrieved June 1, 2006 from http://www.glsen.org/cgi-bin/iowa/educator/library/record/1174.html

MARGARET Fund of the National Women's Law Center. (2005). Title IX facts & myths. Title IX, I exercise my rights. Retrieved May 26, 2006 from

National Organization for Women (NOW). *Talking about affirmative action.* Retrieved November 2, 2005 from http://www.now.org/issues/affirm/talking.html

One Nation/One California. (1997). *English for the children.* Retrieved June 6, 2006 from http://www.onenation.org

PBS. (2004a). *Time and place: Slavery and the making of America.* Retrieved May 26, 2006 from http://www.pbs.org/wnet/slavery/timeline/1739.html

PBS. (2004b). *Time and place: Slavery and the making of America.* Retrieved May 26, 2006 from http://www.pbs.org/wnet/slavery/timeline/1817.html

Stovall, D. (2005). *Communities struggle to make small serve all.* Rethinking Schools Online, 19, 4. Retrieved June 1, 2006 from http://www.rethinkingschools.org/archive/19_04/stru194.shtml

Chester E. Finn, Jr, Diane Ravitch & Thomas B. Fordham Institute Staff. *The mad, mad world of textbook adoption.* Wash. DC: Thomas B. Fordham Institute: September 2004.

RECONSTRUCTION CONCEPTS: GLOSSARY AND ANNOTATED BIBLIOGRAPHY

Nearly every time I teach a class, I have a student who expresses mixture of shock, relief, and hope because they finally have words to understand and work through a belief or notion that has been with them for a long time but sat dormant because they had no framework to work it through. Having a vocabulary, even a minimal vocabulary, for these kinds of notions can be enormously beneficial. When we have the framework we can ask meaningful questions, solve problems, and find answers. As with the other sections, this is not an exhaustive list. Instead, use it as a starting place for your dialogue, a tool for jogging your memory or a place to learn about new things you want to learn about even more. These are less definitions and more so ways to think about a number of important theoretical concepts that intersect with our work and strengthen our critical reflection. Each term is broadly explained with a definition, a source, or a connection to a text and an example of how it might apply in our practice.

Affirmative Action

This term refers to the policies, responses, and legal initiatives that have been put in place to help equalize the imbalance in the playing field that is a result of past and present discrimination. Of the many myths and misunderstandings that surround affirmative action is that these policies are designed only to benefit people of African-American descent. This is false, and in fact, affirmative-action policies are designed to combat discrimination based on gender, race, color, and national origin.

The National Organization for Women is one group that has been especially vocal in the attempts to break down the myth that affirmative action is "reverse discrimination" or "reverse racism." They point out the following misconceptions:

- Affirmative action gives unearned rights to certain people while leaving others out unfairly.
- Affirmative action is no longer necessary because oppressed groups now have equal opportunities and discrimination is illegal.
- Affirmative action should be based on economic need instead of gender or color.
- Affirmative action lowers standards by allowing unqualified candidates into positions that they should not be in.
- Qualified, white, male applicants are being denied admission into schools unfairly because of affirmative action.
- Since other people do not get special consideration when applying to schools or for jobs, women and people of color should not either.
- Affirmative action can only help certain people.
- Affirmative action means preferences.

They encourage us instead to consider the following facts:

- Affirmative action levels the playing field so that everyone has a chance to compete. Nearly 100% of the highest-level corporate jobs are held by white, male individuals.
- Despite gains made by the Civil Rights Movement and Women's Rights Movement, women and people of color still hold significantly fewer professional positions than white men, and they still make significantly less money than white men.
- Women and people of color of every economic class should have the chance to compete for every job. Furthermore, poverty impacts every group differently. And we must consider the correlation between

racial groups and poverty: simply put, there are more impoverished people in minority groups than in dominant cultural groups.

- Affirmative action gives qualified candidates an opportunity to overcome racism and the barriers brought on by racism.
- If half the people of color who are admitted to schools through affirmative-action programs were cut, the acceptance rates for white men would increase only by 2%.
- Many people get special consideration when applying for positions: veterans, athletes, and children of alumni, to name a few.
- Affirmative action helps everyone. Everyone benefits when racism and sexism are eliminated.
- Affirmative action means equal opportunity. (National Organization for Women, 2005)

Having a firm and fluent grasp of the many misconceptions and facts that inform our thinking on affirmative action is especially important as critical educators, because it is often these very misunderstandings that become the backbone to many arguments as to why critical theory is unnecessary and why institutional racism does not exist. Affirmative action has become a buzzword and a scapegoat, and since misunderstandings about affirmative action populate so many misinformed analyses of racism, having an especially firm grasp of the facts that counter the myths allows for increased opportunities to set the record straight.

Afro-Centric

The Afro-centric, or African-centered, worldview is very different from a Eurocentric, or Europe-centered, worldview. Afro-centrism is centered on the beliefs that:

- The highest value of life lies in the interpersonal relationships between people.
- One gains knowledge through symbolic imagery and rhythm.
- One should live in harmony with nature.
- There is a oneness between humans and nature.
- The survival of the group holds the utmost importance.
- People should appropriately utilize the materials around them.
- One's self is complementary to others.

- Change occurs in a natural, evolutionary cycle.
- Spirituality and inner divinities hold the most significance.
- There are a plethora of deities to worship.
- Cooperation, collective responsibility, and interdependence are the key values that all should strive to achieve.
- All people are considered to be equal, share a common bond, and be a part of the group.
- The Afro-centric worldview is a circular one, in which all events are tied together with one another. (Eurocentric and Afrocentric Worldviews, 2005)

It isn't enough to simply name these worldviews; we must question the ways in which each has shaped our own experience and, more important, how each can potentially inform and improve our teaching. Are there times when one is more appropriate or useful? Probably so. William Watkins (2000) tells us, "Eurocentric analysis is viewed as linear. Rooted in empiricism, rationalism, scientific method, and positivism, its aim is prediction and control…African epistemology, on the other hand, is circular…and seeks interpretation, expression, and understanding without preoccupation with verification" (2000, p. 351). The problem is, of course, the privileging of Eurocentric curriculum and content over all others. Decentering Eurocentrism in our schools gives us the opportunity to explore the multitude of ways that other worldviews can help us to become richer, fuller, and more balanced learners, citizens, and human beings.

Ally/accomplice—to be an ally means to outwardly and actively leverage one's privilege to support marginalized groups and dismantle oppression. It's important to stress that there are wrong ways to be an ally. Writer and activist Mia McKenzie explains on her blog called Black Girl Dangerous, "People claim 'ally' for themselves regularly and with ease. But the truth is that being an ally takes more work than most of us imagine. In fact, it takes constant vigilance. And there are many ways we fail at it everyday" (McKenzie, 2015). Hoping to be rewarded for advocating on behalf of marginalized people is not being an ally. Speaking on our behalf is not being an ally. Saving and/or discovering another culture is not being an ally; rather, recognizing how equity for some peoples advances all peoples is the best way to be an ally for all of us.

Assessment

This term refers to the act of evaluating if a student has mastered the skills or content that he or she has been presented with. While this may seem like a neutral enough function, there are certain values that should edify this process for us as critical educators.

Sally Brown, Phil Race, and Brenda Smith (1996) published a book called 500 Tips on Assessment, and a "Ten Point Assessment Manifesto" comes from the last section of that book. Among the many important points for critical educators to consider are these:

- Assessment should be based on an understanding of how students learn and should be a positive part of the learning experience.
- Assessment should accommodate individual learning differences, and a variety of assessment instruments should be utilized in order to accommodate and encourage creativity.
- The purpose and expectations of assessment should be clearly explained. The methods of assessment should be consistent and reliable.
- Students should receive meaningful feedback on their learning and their performance.
- Teachers should use assessment to reflect on their own practices. (FairTest, 2004)

As with standards and standardized tests, there is nothing inherently wrong with assessment, and of course, assessing student performance is one of the most important components of our job. Yet, as with standards, assessment should not be used in a punitive way, and they should be a meaningful and constructive part of the curriculum and learning experience.

Banking Method of Education

The banking method of education is how Paulo Freire (2000) describes pedagogy and practice that is an "act of depositing, in which the students are the depositories, and the teacher is the depositor. Instead of communicating, the teacher issues communiqués and makes deposits which the students patiently receive, memorize, and repeat" (p. 72). Understanding this concept is crucial to understanding the work of Freire and all the work that extends from his as well. The banking method is characterized by these attributes:

- The teacher teaches, and the students are taught.
- The teacher knows everything, and the students know nothing.
- The teacher thinks, and the students are thought about.
- The teacher talks, and the students listen, meekly.
- The teacher disciplines, and the students are disciplined.
- The teacher chooses and enforces a choice, and the students comply.
- The teacher acts, and the students have the illusion of acting through the action of the teacher.
- The teacher chooses the program's content, and the students (who were not consulted) adapt to it.
- The teacher confuses the authority of knowledge with his or her own professional authority, which the teacher sets in opposition to the freedom of the students.
- The teacher is the subject of the learning process, while the pupils are mere objects. (p. 73)

Beyond these conditions, the implications of the banking method are extensive. Freire's indictment is that within this method, the teacher is:

> projecting an absolute ignorance onto others, a characteristic of the ideology of oppression, negates education and knowledge as processes of inquiry. The teacher presents himself to his students as a necessary opposite; by considering their ignorance absolute, he justifies his own existence. The students, alienated like the slave in the Hegelian dialect, accept their ignorance as justifying the teacher's existence—but, unlike the slave, they never discover that they educate the teacher. (2000, p. 72)

Direct instruction, standardized tests, textbooks, and structured curriculum are instruments that reflect the banking method of education, to name just a few.

Classroom-management programs that are strongly behaviorist and heavily reliant on external motivation and rewards reflect the banking method of education. It is, of course, very easy to become dependent on these methods, especially in a school that does not readily support change. Of course, we all exist within systems larger than us over which we have no control. Yet, Freire clearly calls upon us to take our roles seriously and live them aggressively.

Remember, as far as Freire is concerned, we are either for something or against something. He says that "those who use the banking approach, knowingly or unknowingly (for there are innumerable well-intentioned bank-clerk teachers who do not realize they are serving only to dehumanize), fail to perceive that the deposits themselves contain contradictions about reality" (Freire, 2000, p. 75).

Canon

The canon generally refers to the traditional curriculum of literary education, that is, the list of books that people such as E. D. Hirsch believe constitute worthwhile and lasting reading. For most, to define the canon is a rhetorical act; we graduated from high school ourselves, so we know what books make it onto this list and who wrote them.

Therefore, the act of defining the canon is a useful exercise because it puts into relief what is not in the canon. In my experience, this list usually turns out to be extensive, interesting, and reflective of our students and their lives. The challenge as educators is to create our own canon: a canon of books that reflects our lives and the lives of our students. This is a truly interruptive act, because by doing this, we recreate history and transform culture. This is not to say that the books that are already on the list have no usefulness or place in our lives. This is not true. However, they will be more useful to us in the context of a larger body of work that prioritizes the experience of our students instead of marginalizing it.

Circular Thinking

Circular thinking is relational and focuses on interdependencies. Using the research of Asa Hilliard, both Janice Hale and Jawanza Kunjufu have investigated how understanding the difference between circular thinking, which is associated with African-American culture, and linear thinking, which is associated with European culture, can impact our classrooms. The implication here is that children of color bring certain cognitive and epistemological, as well as cultural, differences into the classroom. Forcing children of color to conform to a European, linear, analytic curriculum is setting them up for failure and to receive the message that they are inherently wrong. Furthermore, children of color do bring their own capital to our classrooms. However, since they are forced into a curriculum that is not based on their cognitive styles, and that privileges Western thinking styles, it does not take long for a deficit-model approach to take root. According to Kunjufu (1990), "The objective here is to articulate what those differences are and encourage the advocacy of these different learning styles wherever African-American children are being taught" (p. 38).

Cognition

Cognition is knowing. It is both noun and verb—the act of knowing, the fact that one knows. It is knowledge. What cognition is is remarkably complex and, ironically, further complicated by attempts to define and understand it. How can something be the act of and the fact of at the same time? The attempt to define and speak of cognition is limited by the very borders of language itself. For our purposes, cognition is thinking and knowing. While this definition is wide in scope, ambitious as well as ambiguous, what is important to understand is that the intersection of thinking, knowing, expression and creation will be completely different and personal places for each child. This is further complicated by the intersection of the personal places with all of the external factors: the classroom, the resources, and you, the teacher. In order to be effective educators, we must recognize the intricate existence of these places and intersections.

Is cognition different from intelligence? Is it different from epistemology? Is it different from what an individual child can do with any particular content? Is it where all of these extensions intersect? If it is how our students perceive, think, and communicate—how, essentially, they continually organize and respond to their world—then we must have our own grasp of cognition in order to structure their universe so we can maximize their learning experience.

This means consciously constructing the environment in which they learn so as to be aware that they are responding to everything—visual information, cultural information, social information, emotional information, spatial information, the organization of time, and everything else imaginable.

Understanding cognition helps us to anticipate and plan; it helps us to push the intersections even further. However, the danger in seeking to define and understand cognition is in that the limitations of language (and the limits of our own understanding, individually and collectively) itself may end up becoming devices with which we inadvertently exclude or shortchange our students. Sometimes a particular child, or a particular act or fact of knowing, may not fit our definition or understanding. Be careful not to categorize one act as valid and another as invalid. This is why it is important to expand our own views of what and how one can know and how we place value on these things.

Because so much is new and revealing itself to children, and because they experience such intense leaps and bounds as they grow, consider the possibility that the cognition playground may be a much more dynamic place for children than it is for the adults who teach them. It takes careful planning and discernment to keep up. Careful and deliberate consideration of the perceptual, intellectual, and linguistic abilities, of cognition, must be at work when planning goals and assessment, when choosing resources, and when creating physical environments.

Counterhegemony

To be counterhegemonic is to acknowledge the existence of hegemony and the role it plays in shaping our lives and our work as teachers. But, as Daniel R. Nicholson (1998) tells us in Developing a Media Literacy of Whiteness in Advertising, to be counterhegemonic requires more than awareness; it requires action. He speaks of his own endorsement of a counterhegemonic position and says that practice that is counterhegemonic must meet the following criteria:

- It is work that is educational and reflects an "incessant" effort to educate the population most affected by hegemony.
- Central to its mission is concern for intellectual, moral, cultural, political, and economic change.
- Counterhegemonic groups must develop counterinstitutions, ideologies, and cultures that provide an ethical alternative and a lived example of how the world can be different.
- These forces must work to confuse and thwart consensus and develop conditions that nurture the struggle toward a balanced social order.
- They must seek to enter and influence individual consciousness and the disjuncture between received versions of reality and lived contradictions. (p. 194)

Being counterhegemonic means moving beyond awareness to execute a deliberate and intentional plan of action that involves, first and foremost, making choices. We make choices about what we teach and how we are going to present that material. Even with material that is mandated and about which we have no choice, we can still present that material in a certain context that is in keeping with our counterhegemonic objectives. We make choices about where we teach and whom we teach. Staying true to our counterhegemonic objectives may mean delivering messages and bringing different things to light, depending on which community or cultural group we work with. And remember, no change can happen in isolation, and these counterhegemonic changes can and must take place in every community. Lastly, we make choices about why we teach. If we agree that the classroom is the most fertile environment for change of this nature, then our reasons for teaching should be born of this shared understanding.

Critical Multiculturalism

Joe Kincheloe and Shirley Steinberg (1997) help us to do this in their *Changing Multiculturalism*. They define critical multiculturalism as being "dedicated to the notion of egalitarianism and the elimination of human suffering" (p. 24). "Critical multiculturalists attempt to expose the subtle and often hidden educational processes that privilege the already affluent and undermine the efforts of the poor" (p. 25). Beyond this, another important theme of critical multiculturalism involves the way power shapes our consciousness. Such a process involves the processes by which ideological inscriptions are imprinted on subjectivity, the ways desire is mobilized by power forces for hegemonic outcomes, the means by which discursive powers shape thinking and behavior through both the presences and absences of different words and concepts, and the methods by which individuals assert their agency and self-direction in relationship to such power plays (p. 25).

Critical multiculturalism is performative in that it is defined by the act of the teacher positioning himself or herself in a certain way and presenting his or her curriculum in a certain way so that the teacher does not make the mistake that Kincheloe and Steinberg define as working in "complicity with cultural reproduction" (p. 26).

When E. D. Hirsch (1987) wrote *Cultural Literacy*, he was centralizing a body of Western ideas, individuals, and texts as legitimate knowledge. Kwame Anthony Appiah and Henry Louis Gates (1996) wrote *The Dictionary of Global Culture* as a way to decenter Hirsch's work. Similarly, the book

Measured Lies: The Bell Curve Examined (Kincheloe, Steinberg, & Gresson, 1996) decenters the agenda of The Bell Curve, which attempted to prove that children of certain races were unable to learn, so attempting to teach them was a waste of time and resources.

But we don't need to write a book in order to decenter the content and standards that have found their way into the whole of our schools. In fact, teaching a rap song, for instance, as poetry not only decenters what we traditionally name as legitimate literature, but forces us to consider and value that song as legitimate art.

Critical Pedagogy

In the essay entitled "Developing a Curriculum and Critical Pedagogy," Leila E. Villaverde (2004, pp. 131–135) presents how critical pedagogy can be distinguished by the following characteristics:

- Understanding the reality that curriculum goes beyond what the packaged or standardized "curriculum" consists of and also involves teacher experience and perception, interaction with peers, and life in general.
- Teachers should want students to be independent learners.
- Attention will be paid to the implicit curriculum.
- Questioning is the core of the curriculum, not just for the sake of questioning, but to deepen knowledge, engage and critique multiple discourses, and transform ideas into action and into more equitable experiences for those involved.
- The motivation stems from a recognition that schooling is an agent of social change, and the learning students acquire can transform their lives and the lives of others.
- The pedagogy analyzes and exposes the dominant value systems that shape the way knowledge is defined and curriculum is constructed and tested.
- The pedagogy sees knowledge everywhere, not just in school.
- Dialogue and reflection are key components.

Of course, critical pedagogy may manifest itself much differently from classroom to classroom depending on demographics and other factors. Regardless of the externals, these characteristics should set the foundation for every classroom and learning experience that we provide for our students.

Critical Theory

Funny though it may seem, I could write an entire volume on critical theory and never once use these specific words. Metaphorically, it is like canvas to the painting: You could teach a class about painting and never have to mention the canvas; it is assumed and understood. To me, there is no education without critical theory, and whether or not they strongly identify with it, every educator must wrestle with and define it for themselves. According to Joe Kincheloe and Peter McLaren (2000), "We can be against critical theory or for it, but, especially at the present historical juncture, we cannot be without it" (p. 279).

Still, semantically, the term is often misunderstood. It is not to be confused with being critical, although critical theory is often critical. And it is not to be confused with critical-thinking skills, although understanding of critical theory requires critical thinking skills. With its origins with the Frankfurt School in Germany, critical theory is closely associated with the work of Max Horkheimer, Theodor Odorno, and Herbert Marcuse.

For the purposes of this text and to have a common working definition, I think it is best to turn again to the work of Kincheloe and McLaren (2000): "…Critical theory analyzes competing power interests between groups and individuals within a society—identifying who gains and who loses in specific situations" (p. 281).

Critical-Thinking Skills

In one context, perhaps the most recognizable context, critical-thinking skills will refer to thinking beyond content. Critical-thinking skills can be interchangeable with higher-order thinking skills, which are interchangeable with Bloom's Taxonomy of the Cognitive Domain. There is nothing inherently wrong with critical thinking or moving beyond content; however, we must be cautious when "what often masquerades as critical thinking in most classrooms is a set of prescriptive steps and practices that may reflect important processes, but are attached to relatively inane content" (Ladson-Billings, 2000, p. 5). In the article entitled "Teaching in Dangerous Times," which Gloria Ladson-Billings (2000) wrote for Re-thinking Schools, she suggests instead that we move toward "sociopolitical consciousness," which is thinking that moves beyond vicarious knowledge into the spaces of meaningful activity and action (p. 5).

Cultural Capital

According to Michael Apple (1990), cultural capital can be defined as "cultural events and artifacts," "social action or activity—with education as a particular form of that activity—as tied to a larger arrangement of institutions which apportion resources so that particular groups and classes have historically been helped while others have been less adequately treated" (p. 10). Cultural capital is a currency that those with possession can trade in for other resources. For instance, the knowledge of the game of golf can be traded in to gain entry to certain social circles. Being a part of these circles can be used as currency to garner other resources and so on. It is the dominant culture that possesses the most cultural capital, and therefore, the body of capital will reflect and privilege the dominant culture. Schools and other cultural institutions are keepers of this information and are charged with the manufacturing and transmission of this information.

Cultural Literacy

According to E. D. Hirsch (1987), cultural literacy is possession of the "basic information needed to thrive in the modern world" (p. xiii). The notion of a cultural literacy is, at best, problematic because someone or some group must determine what this information is. There is no way for this determination to be made without privileging the experience of one culture or cultural group over another. Hirsch has generously stepped up to be the one to make this determination. On the first page of his preface, Hirsch claims that his "cultural literacy constitutes the only one sure avenue of opportunity for disadvantaged children" (p. xiii). He goes on to say that "the basic goal of education in a human community is acculturation, the transmission to children of the specific information shared by the adults of the group" (p. xvi). The idea that the only hope for disadvantaged children is for them to be acculturated into his, or any, static notion of what constitutes the "basic information" is absurd and goes against everything that we know about empowering children with the tools of their own culture.

The reason it is important to be aware of this term and of this phenomenon is because it is very easy for well-meaning educators to fall into Hirsch's trap if they have not come to a place in their own practice where they can ask, "Whose knowledge and for what?" It is very important to be skeptical of any attempt to draw lines around what knowledge can or cannot be.

Cultural Proficiency

Cultural proficiency is "esteeming culture; knowing how to learn about individual and organizational culture; interaction effectively in a variety of cultural environments" (p. 31). For teachers, to be culturally proficient means to always be learning about the students we teach and to do so in a way that doesn't mock or "other-ize" them, but rather helps us to incorporate our increasing knowledge about their lives into our instruction and interaction with them. This means ongoing examination of our expectations, actions, and reactions.

In addition, we need to teach our students to be culturally proficient, which means teaching them "economic English" or cultural habits or behaviors that we can say typically belong to dominant culture, so that they will be able to code-switch when they need to in order to function in the world outside of your classroom. It also means teaching this in a way that recognizes the strengths and necessity of both codes, without approaching the students' code from a place of condemnation or disrespect. It is probably impossible to become completely free of bias, of preference, or the need to build community with our own cultural peers. I believe a more realistic and honorable goal is to become culturally proficient, so that we are constantly interacting respectfully, while learning and growing in the process.

Curriculum

This term is broadly used to describe the content of what we learn and what we teach. I refer to Arthur Wellesley Foshay (2000):

> The curriculum is often defined as the summation of one's experience. From this viewpoint there is the school curriculum, which concerns us here, and the life curriculum, which includes all of one's experiences. To view the school curriculum as the summation of all of one's experience is at once to recognize its complexity. Because experience is an individual affair, each person's school curriculum is unique. Because one's school curriculum includes all school experience, there is no logical way to put boundaries around it. Because the life curriculum deals with one's entire life, it, too, is boundless. The curriculum is as boundless as the universe of experience. (p. 1)

It is helpful for the educator to think beyond the "written curriculum" or even the "taught" curriculum and instead conceive of the curriculum as the entire individual experience. This way, we can begin to close the gap between the reality of standards, written objectives, programs of study, and even our text-books and prepackaged classroom materials and the seemingly idealized tenets of critical theory. Remembering that the curriculum is the entire experience helps us to incorporate theory so that it can inform our teaching. It also helps us to break down the artificial walls of the classroom and treat education as a synthesized happening rather than one that is removed or set apart from the rest of our students' lives. Since the curriculum is all school experience, what follows is that the student's whole life and complete experience are brought with him or her into the classroom. This is a tool for the educator, because it creates a new possibility for expanded and more authentic connections between the students and what is being taught.

Decentering

To center is to place something—an idea, a content, an action—as central, as the object of focus. So, to decenter is to shift something—the idea, content, or action—away from the center. This is an especially important act for teachers who see themselves as disruptive because often our work is to shift the typically accepted methodologies and "legitimate knowledge" away from the center of our own and our students' learning experiences.

David Geoffrey Smith (1996) tells us that "in the field of education, especially curriculum studies, the decentering of the West has meant widespread reevaluation of the central canons and oeuvres that have defined school and university programs to this point, with a bringing forward of what has been systematically excluded in the 'standard' works of the tradition as taught" (p. 462).

The act of decentering, while seeming somewhat subtle, is actually a significant part of what critical theorists and educators do.

Deficit Model

If you have ever heard a teacher say, "These kids can't…," then you are already familiar with the deficit model.

According to Craig Sautter (1994), "For urban kids, environmental risks are all too easily translated into student deficits. And attempts by policymakers, educators, and researchers to 'overcome' these deficits gradually have developed into a negative picture of poor and minority children and youth. This deficit model has dominated education for the supposedly at-risk." The deficit model is possible because notions, such as cultural literacy, privilege a certain body of knowledge and skills over another. Understanding and dismantling any deficit-model beliefs about students are the first and most important steps that any new teacher must take. Instead of approaching urban students from a deficit model, Asa Hilliard suggests we look at the qualities that urban (in his particular study, African-American) students bring to the classroom, qualities such as a preference for inferential reasoning and a high proficiency for nonverbal communication, as strengths and build our curriculum around these qualities (Hale, 1982, p. 4).

Ebonics

From The Real Ebonics Debate (paraphrased):

> The term Ebonics was coined in January 1973 by Dr. Robert L. Williams, during a small-group discussion at a conference. Etymologically, Ebonics is a compound of two words: ebony (black) and phonics (sounds). Thus, Ebonics literally means black sounds. As an all-encompassing, nonpejorative label, the term refers to the language of the West African, Caribbean, and American slave descendants of Niger-Congo African origin.

Ebonics includes both the verbal and paralinguistic communications of African-American people; this means that Ebonics represents an underlying psychological thought process. The phrase African-American Vernacular is a more appropriate and effective descriptor for communicating all of this. The nonverbal sounds, cues, gestures, and so on that are systematically used in the process of communication by African-American people are encompassed by this term as well.

This term gives us a spacious opportunity to examine the differences among the intended meaning, the so-called neutral meaning, and the manipulated meaning of words. Consider the weight and complexity of this term and the background required to fully grasp its intended meaning. Then, imagine the power this word can carry if the intended meaning is manipulated to accomplish a different purpose.

Code-switching is also a term with tremendous dimension. It refers to the ability of bilingual individuals to switch between their languages depending on the appropriateness of a given situation. This, of course, refers to the necessary change in all of the nonverbal, cultural, and psychological components as well (Perry & Delpit, 1998).

Epistemology

Epistemology is the branch of philosophy that deals with the nature of knowledge: How is it that we know?

The understanding of epistemology is important to us as critical teachers and learners because it validates that different people know things in different ways; while each can be unique unto itself, each can be valid. This opens up many new possibilities that don't exist within our typically positivistic and traditional educational institutions.

Shulamit Reinharz (1992) is the author of Feminist Methods in Social Research. In the chapter "Original Feminist Research Methods," she discusses the work of Susan Griffin and her book Woman and Nature: The Roaring Inside Her. Quoting Griffin:

> I found that I could best discover my insights about the logic of civilized man by going underneath logic, that is by writing associatively and thus enlisting my intuition, or uncivilized self...One of the loudest complaints this book makes about patriarchal thought (or the thought of civilized man) is that it claims to be objective, and separated from emotion, and so it is appropriate that the style of this book does not make that separation. (p. 231)

Allowing herself access to her uncivilized self or her intuition was allowing herself access to a different epistemology: one that is different from the voice of patriarchal, civilized man that seemed to deny it. Here we can see that understanding and allowing for different epistemologies can create new opportunities for learning and building meaning.

Essentialism

C. McCarthy describes essentialism as the tendency "to treat social groups as stable or homogenous entities" (1993, p. xv). "Racial groups such as 'Asians,' 'Latinos,' or 'blacks' are therefore discussed as though members of these groups possessed some innate and invariant characteristics that set them apart from each other and from 'whites.' The consequence of essentialism is that the 'noise' of 'multidimensionality, historic variability, and subjectivity' is eliminated from the discussion of difference in society and in education" (McCarthy & Crichlow, 1993, p. xv). Essentialism in the classroom can cause us to miss out on the opportunity for each child to fully experience his or her own curriculum. It can cause us to miss out on the many different and individual points of intersection with each child and his or her experience of the classroom or the text.

Eurocentric

Eurocentricism refers to thought, action, or perception that is shaped by a European worldview or experience. According to Eurocenteric and Afro-centric worldviews, Eurocentrism is characterized by a worldview centered around the beliefs that:

- The highest value of life lies in the object, or in the acquisition of the object.
- One gains knowledge through counting and measuring.
- One should control and dominate nature.
- There is a dichotomy, or separateness, between nature and humans.
- The survival of the fittest holds the utmost importance.
- People should have an unlimited exploitation of the materials around them.
- One's self is distinct from others.
- Change occurs to meet the immediate objectives and is quite arbitrary.
- A distant, impersonal god holds the most significance.
- There is only one supreme deity to worship.
- Competition, independence, separateness, and individual rights are the key values that all should strive to achieve.
- All people are considered to be individualistic, unique, and different.
- The Eurocentric worldview is a linear one, in which all events are separate and there is no togetherness. (p. 1)

Feminism

Simply put, feminism is the desire for social and economic equality between the sexes. Feminism is also the term used to describe the political movement based around these beliefs, especially in reference to the Women's Movement of the 1960s. What is not quite as simple, and comes as a complete surprise to most, is that young people, especially young women, may have a very negative understanding of the idea of feminism and may be very opposed to the idea of identifying themselves as feminists. It is not uncommon for our students to associate feminism with "man-hating" or some notion of desexualization or forced homosexuality.

Our task as educators, then, becomes to dismantle this understanding and encourage our students to embrace an authentic understanding of feminism and to see why it is valuable for them to do so. In her essay "Fear of Feminism," Lisa Maria Hogeland (1994) suggests we offer a different version of feminism to our students: "At its best, the feminist challenging of individualism, of narrow notions of freedom, is transformative, exhilarating, empowering" (p. 7). She says:

> feminism offers an arena for selfhood beyond personal relationships, but not discon-
> nected from them. It offers—and requires—courage, intelligence, boldness, sensitiv-
> ity, relationality, complexity, a sense of purpose, and lest we forget, a sense of humor
> as well. (p. 7)

Ghetto

From Wikipedia:

> A ghetto is an area where people from a specific ethnic background or united in a
> given culture or religion live as a group, voluntarily or involuntarily, in milder or
> stricter seclusion. The word historically referred to restricted housing zones for Jews;
> however, it now commonly labels any poverty-stricken urban area. (p. 1)

Disrupting this definition is incredibly important because this word is almost exclusively used to describe people of color that live in urban areas. But if we unpack this definition, then the most expensive, exclusive neighborhood of any city or suburb could be and is a ghetto as well. This, I hope, will force us to examine our own experience and look at the ways in which voluntary or invol-untary seclusion inform our choices and how we see others and their choices. This is the fluid and transitory nature of language, especially slang, which tends to be even more immediate and alive. In keeping, ghetto is a term that has tremendous negative connotations and currency. However, as we come to learn more about the complexity and constructive attributes of the urban areas that our students may live in, we'll see that even the most common use of this word is itself complex. This word can inspire pride as much as shame. A word like ghetto challenges us to see that while every human being deserves adequate housing, safety, and a beautiful place to call home, the places that we know as ghettos consist of complex family structures and personal histories. The places we know as ghettos are composed of children and families that are resourceful, tightly knit, and organized. As educators, we are often faced with dualities like this. Recognizing this complexity will help us to establish genuine and productive relationships with our students that have our humanity and our similarities as a foundation.

Giftedness

Generally speaking, gifted is the term used to describe individuals with exceptional skills, be they mathematical, scientific, musical, within the visual arts, or social. These are some characteristics of gifted children:

- Advanced social maturity
- Advanced moral reasoning
- Sensitivity
- Asynchronous development
- Perfectionism
- Strong conceptual thinking
- Fast learners
- Desire for solitude
- Preference for complexity
- Concerns about issues of morality, justice, spirituality

Some research connects giftedness to physical injury and to other "negative stresses." The deficit in one area can result in an increase of ability in another. This can serve to dramatically reshape our view of teaching and our students. Some research shows that exposure to traumatic experiences can result in an increase in certain brain activity. Does this mean that instead of perceiving children who are "at risk" or that come from certain backgrounds as unteachable or worse, we can perceive them as potentially gifted and potentially exceptional? It does if we are willing to extend our view and our values in terms of what they are exceptional at. It does if we are willing to take a complex view of standards and intelligence and realize that the things some students may be gifted at are not necessarily the same talents measured by standardized tests and typical curricular models.

Hegemony

Hegemony is a whole body of practices and expectations; our assignments of energy, our ordinary understanding of man and his world. It is a set of meanings and values which, as they are experienced as practices, appear as reciprocally confirming (Apple, 1990, p. 5).

Hegemony is a concept that comes from the work of Antonio Gramsci and is more fully developed by Raymond Williams and Michael Apple. Williams says that understanding "the notion of hegemony as deeply saturating the consciousness of a society seems to be fundamental" (Apple, 1990, p. 5).

Gramsci himself was concerned with institutional power relationships within Marxism and capitalism. He believed that human agency played the greatest role in historical change. He believed that those in power stayed in power because of their hold on economic institutions as well as intellectual and moral institutions.

> ...Dominant groups in society, including fundamentally but not exclusively the ruling class, maintain their dominance by securing the 'spontaneous consent' of subordinate groups, including the working class, through the negotiated construction of a political and ideological consensus which incorporates both dominant and dominated groups. (Strinati, 1995, p. 153)

Many thinkers such as Noam Chomsky believe that hegemony is a more effective means of control and oppression than actual physical force, because if you control the minds of a group of people, control of the body will follow. This consent is what we hope to teach our students to recognize and work against. It is what we seek to interrupt instead of reproduce in our own schools and work.

Hidden Curriculum

If we accept the premise that hegemony exists and that schools play a primary role in producing and maintaining hegemony, then we can understand that the hidden curriculum is "the tacit teaching to students of norms, values, and dispositions that goes on simply by their living in and coping with the institutional expectations and routines of schools day in and day out for a number of years" (Apple, 1990, p. 44). "The norms and values that are implicitly, but effectively, taught in schools and that are not usually talked about in teachers' statements of ends or goals" (Apple, 1990, p. 44). We don't need to look far to find examples of the hidden curriculum. Perhaps the most overt is that it is required for most students to recite the Pledge of Allegiance before they are old enough to comprehend the meaning of the words. There are more subtle examples in all of our schools. It is the subtle and less easily detectable examples that make it possible for the hidden curriculum to function as ubiquitously as it does.

Institutional Racism

In his essay entitled "Race and Social Theory," Cornell West (1999) examines the different constructs of the phenomena of racism. He tells us that the "very category of 'race'—denoting primarily skin color—was first employed as a means of classifying human bodies by Francois Bernier, a French physician. This first substantial racial division of humankind appeared in the influential Natural System (1735) by the preeminent naturalist of the 18th century, Carolus Linnaeus" (p. 259). He goes on to tell us that "both instances reveal racist practices—in that both degrade and devalue non-Europeans—and the level of intellectual codification" (p. 259). We can see then that from the earliest points in history, race functions as a tool to separate and subjugate people. Different from personal racism, the act of one individual harming another because of skin color, institutional racism occurs when race is scientifically (as in the above example) or systematically delineated (as in law or public policy) in order to privilege certain groups and hurt other groups.

Giving Whiteness a Black Eye, an interview with Ronald Chennault and Michael Eric Dyson, scrutinizes the contrast of this, saying that we must come to terms with "whiteness as institution" as well (Chennault, 1998, p. 300). The implications for us as educators are tremendous. We must come to terms with how we have contributed to, been hurt by, and benefited from institutionally racist practices. We must also do the work to measure how racism (and sexism and classism) work themselves out in our schools and classrooms through our curriculum, methodology, and content choices.

Legitimate Knowledge

This is the term Michael Apple uses to refer to the body of knowledge and also the epistemology—not just what we know, but how we know—that is ordained and validated by hegemonic forces. This term is on our side—and it functions to warn us that whatever content or knowledge it describes is in support of those forces. This knowledge will have certain characteristics: It is measurable, standardized, consumable and static. It is list-able. This is nowhere nearly as perfectly done than in E. D. Hirsch's series of books entitled Cultural Literacy.

Linear/Circular Thinking

Linear thinking is analytic and builds upon itself from one point to the next. Using the research of Asa Hilliard, both Janice Hale and Jawanza Kunjufu have investigated how understanding the difference between circular thinking, which is associated with African-American culture, and linear thinking, which is associated with European culture, can impact our classrooms. The implication here is that children of color bring certain cognitive and epistemological, as well as cultural, differences into the classroom. Forcing children of color to conform to a European, linear, analytic curriculum is setting them up for failure and to receive the message that they are inherently wrong. Furthermore, children of color do bring their own capital to our classrooms. However, since they are forced into a curriculum that is not based on their cognitive styles and that privileges Western thinking styles, it does not take long for a deficit-model approach to take root. According to Kunjufu (1990), "The objective here is to articulate what those differences are and encourage the advocacy of these different learning styles wherever African-American children are being taught" (p. 38).

Literacy

In their essay entitled "Gaining Access to Critical Literacy: Rethinking the Role of Reading Programs," Herman S. Garcia and Teresa Valenzuela (2004) suggest a different way to conceptualize literacy (paraphrased):

- Literacy must be contextualized within the social/political dynamics of the students' lives.
- Literacy must go beyond decoding letters and mechanical skills.
- Literacy is not neutral and not a basic skill. Literacy includes a relationship "in which learners can mediate the struggle for emancipation, democracy, social justice, and transformative practices."

- Cultural proficiency and "cultural literacy" are tools for students to "embrace and understand aspects of dominant culture that will provide a basis for transformation of wider social order."
- "It is important to master the dominant language for accessing the wider world, but not at the expense of individual identities."
- Children must not be silenced. Literacy must not be taught in a "banking system" but rather in a "problem-posing" system so that teacher and student work together to build meaning.
- Literacy is the most crucial component in a student's success or failure in school. The literacy program will empower students. (p. 279)

This shapes our work as educators, chiefly by forcing us to look beyond the mechanics of literacy to the bigger implications and possibilities. It also forces us to suspend the authority of text and curricular materials to include the student in the process of meaning-making. When students are involved in the process of meaning-making, they will be encouraged to master the mechanical skills that are necessary to make this happen.

Marginalize

In order for something to be forced into the center, something else must be forced out. As stated before, everything else that is not "centered" is relegated to the margins.

In his study entitled "The Technologies of Marginality," Glenn M. Hudak (1993), using the work of bell hooks to construct his thesis, conducted a "microstudy" of two college-bound high-school boys. Hudak is able to "map out the terrain of marginality" by working closely with the two boys, "both defining themselves as being on the margins of school life; each presenting a different map of marginality" (p. 178).

Hudak goes on eloquently to tell us "The margin, however, cannot be viewed solely as a site of exclusion and repression, as a place to which one is marginalized due to one's race, class, gender, or sexual preference. To be sure, marginalization is a practice of oppression." However, the margin can also be a site of resistance.

By locating oneself in the margins, one refuses to forget the past, and instead keeps its memory alive. When memory is politicized, the margins come to represent a social location that is on one hand, a place of "deprivation," and on the other "a particular way of seeing reality" whose intent is survival and resistance (1990, p. 153).

I think it is important to note that while we can make the distinction and can certainly look to the margins as a space of renewal and resistance, indeed, this is what it means to use the "tools of the master" to dismantle his house. This does not change the fact that what is located in the margins is determined by what is in the center, which is determined by the oppressive forces. Susan H. Edgerton (1993) tell us that the ways in which groups, individuals, and ideas come to be marginalized in a given culture, society, and/or place has much to do with what is considered to be knowledge and who is considered to possess it. Who is perceived as knower and who is perceived as known. Clearly education is deeply implicated in these processes (p. 223).

Still, even thinking of the margins as a place of refuge is in itself a process that decenters. Remember how Peggy McIntosh (1998) told us that "whites are taught to think of their lives as morally neutral, normative, and average, and also ideal" (p. 1)? Well, consider the possibilities of decentering this myth and instead placing the experiences, the cultures, and the epistemologies of others as the norm and the ideal—not merely tolerable, but ideal.

Paulo Freire (2000) says:

> The oppressed are not "marginals," are not people living "outside" society. They have always been "inside"—inside the structure, which made them "beings for others." The solution is not to "integrate" them into the structure of oppression, but to transform the structure so that they can become "beings for themselves." (p. 79)

Meritocracy

The theory of meritocracy comes from a family of ennobled and well-intentioned theories that represent human beings at their best and with the most potential. We love the belief and hope for humankind that these theories hold for us.

Charles W. Eliot was the president of Harvard and a very influential educator in the early 1900s. He believed that a school's potential to contribute to society lay in its ability to educate each student at what he or she could do best. Out of such an educational program, an educational ladder would emerge, and those with the most talent and most aptitude would climb it. This is a meritocracy: the belief that we start equal, and the cream always rises to the top (Tozer, Senese & Violas, 1998, p. 114).

Theories such as meritocracy, while seemingly well intentioned and benign, can conveniently ignore institutions such as slavery, segregation, legalized sexism, and classism. The effect of these beliefs is that it becomes possible, and completely functional, to maintain and reproduce hegemonic conditions because the source of insufficiency and inferiority must be a flaw within the particular group being oppressed and not the social and economic conditions that make it possible to oppress that group. H. Richard Milner (2010) tells us "When educators approach their work through meritocratic lenses they believe that student performance is primarily a function of hard work, skill, intelligence and persistence. Many factors beyond merit shape students' academic and social success" (p. 15).

Minority

This term is used in the U.S. to name the smaller, nonwhite, cultural, ethnic, and racial groups that make up our population. In this country, the minority groups are African-Americans, Latinos, and Asian Americans (see U.S. census). In scientific, neutral terms, minority, like other terms used to delineate race or ethnicity, is seemingly declarative and benign.

However, intrinsic in the definition of minority is a positioning: Not only is the group smaller in number, but it is defined by the relationship to the bigger, majority group. In the same way that white is not considered a race but the neutral template or standard by which other groups are defined, the majority is considered to be the bar by which other groups get their hue. Not only are the majority groups the smaller groups, but they are also considered less by majority standards. Minority is also a dangerous term because it groups all nonwhite groups together and positions them as outside the majority, despite significant and meaningful differences.

Multiculturalism

In the Glossary of Multicultural Education, James A. and Cherry McGee Banks (1999) define multiculturalism as:

> a philosophical position and movement that assumes that the gender, ethnic, racial, and cultural diversity of a pluralistic society should be reflected in all of the institutionalized structures of educational institutions, including the staff, the norms, and values, the curriculum, and the student body. (p. 430)

While this term has been appropriated to mean many different things along the way, the important thing is that as educators, we must practice critical and responsible multiculturalism.

The necessary work is to go beyond mentions, beyond food fairs and history months to make multiculturalism a starting point for exploring issues of representation and equity. Educators also need to do the work of determining what multiculturalism means for their particular community and how to best recognize, affirm and empower the students and school culture. Every school, every community has its own set of needs and s own potential to grow and empower within a multicultural framework. Responsible, critical, multiculturalism is situated within the context of the school and includes content integration, equity pedagogy and different ways of constructing knowledge to best serve and empower all of the school and community. Culminating with a treasure hunt in a South Asian community where we were instructed to find people from different religions and cross each kind of person off of a list. Looking back, this is deeply problematic on many levels. First, the objectifying and otherizing of the people that this kind of activity involves is disrespectful does nothing to uproot or confront the bias and stereotyping that multiculturalism should combat. Superficially, it felt like we were having fun and exploring our city. I didn't yet have the skills to examine why the class and the culminating trip was so problematic. Sadly, the memory I have that most stands out from this trip was the daughter of one of the two white women who taught the class, running out of the grocery store pretending to vomit because she was so thrown off by the smells from the different spices. Later, as my own analysis would evolve, I amused myself with imagining a group of South Asian graduate students doing a treasure hunt in one of the predominantly white neighborhoods of Chicago. While, this exercise helps to alleviate my own discomfort with my role in this foolishness, the truth is this class was a huge missed learning opportunity. Instead of a treasure hunt we could have focused on schools that serve southeast communities and explored different ways to integrate their culture into our own curriculum so that school is a source of empowerment for these communities. We could have spent this time focusing on the schools in the communities we would more likely have ended up teaching in and instead being spectators in the communities, we could have invited family members and community leaders to address our class and learned from them in a way that would be beneficial to everyone.

Pan-Africanism

John Henrick Clarke (1994) tells us that "in essence, Pan-Africanism is about the restoration of African people to their proper place in world history." He goes further to tell us that "the objective of Pan-Africanism is not only the restoration of land and nationhood: it has as one of its aims the restoration of respect" (p. 1).

Generally referred to as the movement to relearn and restore a connection to the African continent, Pan-Africanism is significant to us as educators because it decenters Europeanism as the principal history that everything else revolves around. Helping all our students, not just students of African descent, to understand and contextualize the rich contributions that Africans and all participators in history have made will help them form stronger identities and have a better sense of their place in the world.

Patriarchy

Patriarchy is a term used to refer to male domination in cultural and personal spaces. The brilliance of patriarchy, like all other forms of domination, is that it does not require a male presence to maintain and reproduce itself. Most schools and school systems are excellent examples of how this can play out. While the profession of teaching is composed almost entirely of women, the highest-paying jobs are still occupied by men, and even worse, our curriculum and pedagogy still privilege the male experience. The point is not to privilege the experience of women over men and create an equally unbalanced system. The point is to examine the ways in which patriarchy informs our actions as teachers so that we can change this and create an equal and democratic learning environment.

Pedagogy

Pedagogy is the term used to describe the art or the craft of teaching. This term can be a mouthful, but rightfully so, as it is responsible for representing a complex and faceted machinery. The true definition of pedagogy evolves as the machinery evolves. But at the root, we can understand this term to involve itself with the production and transmission of knowledge.

In the abstract, pedagogy can be concerned with the processes of meaning-making, choices about learning, and the transmission of culture and values. But in the concrete and day to day, pedagogy can be used to describe a choice of method: If a teacher decides to present a lesson in the form of learning centers instead of whole-group instruction that is a pedagogical choice.

Still, while pedagogy is a useful term because it gives shape to the very fluid character of our craft, it can be somewhat difficult to grasp because of this fluid nature. Riana St. Classis (2003) tells us that there is a special difficulty in writing about pedagogy, for its domain is inside the human mind. One can describe the objects used to facilitate it; one can describe the concepts at which particular pedagogies are driving; one can describe its effects; but pedagogy itself can only be experienced as the reliving of a discovery (p. 2).

So thus the term evolves, depending on the circumstances of discovery.

The etymology of the word comes from the Greek word paidagogas, which is derived from the word for slave (pais) who leads (agogas) the children (also pais) to school, and then comes to mean the mode of instruction itself (St. Classis, 2003, p. 2). So pedagogy is the process of he or she who is the slave to knowledge, the slave to truth, leading the children to the place of learning. We are equal in this process, and we are, neither one of us, ever finished. We never arrive, as there is always something new for us to learn.

In explaining the problem-posing method of education, Paulo Freire (2000) says that we must break with the vertical patterns of education in order to be teacher-students with student-teachers, thus becoming jointly responsible in the process in which all grow (p. 3).

It is within this process that we most experience the fluidity of our work. Embracing a term such as pedagogy helps us to understand and reflect upon this process, this continual discovery, in order to get better at it and to transform our work as well.

Politically Correct

To be politically correct means to be inoffensive. It means to consider equity with respect to naming and representing diverse groups and individuals. The term has become mitigated to become a justification for silencing difficult discussions. The term also comes under fire quite a bit because some believe it censors them and that the real problem is the oversensitivity of the person that finds the language objectionable. Author and activist Klee Bennaly advocates for a shift in perspective, however:

If we consider that often the first and most powerful way we have to act as an ally is to honor the details as to how to pronounce a name or respecting how one chooses to be identified. Be respectful with our thinking and language choices might be the greatest thing we can do while also requiring the least amount of effort. (Bennaly, 2014)

Praxis

Praxis is the act of connecting theory to practice. But as with everything else, it is much more complicated than that. Here is Freire's (2000) equation:

Action

} word=work=praxis
Reflection (p. 87)

He tells us:

As we attempt to analyze dialogue as human phenomenon, we discover something which is the essence of dialogue itself: the word. But the word is more than just an instrument which makes dialogue possible; accordingly, we must seek its constitutive elements. Within the word we find two dimensions, reflection and action, in such radical interaction that if one is sacrificed—even in part—the other immediately suffers. There is no true word that is not at the same time a praxis. Thus, to speak a true word is to transform the world. (p. 87)

Praxis is a process through which we question and then act and then become aware or conscious, so that we may continue to question and act. This process is central to the problem-posing method and to liberatory education.

For Freire, this process is also central to our humanity: "apart from inquiry, apart from praxis, individuals cannot be truly human" (p. 87).

Problem-Posing Method of Education

Freire (2000) says that we must recognize that the construction of reality is a process to which we all contribute. We must instead fully embrace the problem-posing method of education. This involves the abandonment of the banking method and replacing it with posing the "problems of human beings in their relations with the world" (p. 84). This pedagogy and practice differ from the banking method: "Whereas banking education anesthetizes and inhibits creative power, problem-posing education involves a constant unveiling of reality" (p. 84).

This method is also characterized by these attributes:

- It is liberatory and consists of acts of cognition, not transferrals of information.
- Responding to the essence of consciousness—intentionally—rejects communiqués and embodies communication.
- It epitomizes the characteristics of consciousness: being conscious of—not only as intent on objects but as turned in upon itself in a Jasperian split—consciousness as consciousness of consciousness.
- It breaks with the vertical patterns characteristic of banking education and can fulfill its function as the practice of freedom only if it overcomes the teacher-student contradiction. The teacher-of-students and the students-of-teachers cease to exist, and a new term emerges: teacher-student with student-teachers. They become jointly responsible for the process in which all grow.
- The problem-posing educator constantly re-forms his or her reflections in the reflection of the students.
- Students, as they are increasingly posed with problems relating to themselves in the world and with the world, feel increasingly challenged and obliged to respond to that challenge.
- In problem-posing education, people develop their power to perceive critically the way they exist in the world with which and in which they find themselves; they come to see the world not as static reality, but as reality in process, in transformation. (p. 83)

For most of us to adopt a problem-posing pedagogy means that we must uproot our very notions about who the teacher is and who the student is as well. Then we allow that change to inform every choice we make about why, what, and how we teach. My own experience tells me this first step won't be difficult. I often hear teachers reflect on how much they have learned from and have been changed by their students. This method holds incredible hope and possibility for the student and the teacher. When we understand this, we can see how many reasons we have to be hopeful.

Race

Let us consider our discussion of what race is by first considering what race is not. Race is not static, and it is not fixed. In the introduction to Race, Identity and Representation in Education, Cameron McCarthey and Warren Chrichlow (1993) tell us that:

> the challenge before us is to move beyond tendencies to treat race as a stable measurable deposit or category. Racial difference is to be understood as a subject position that can only be defined in what Homi Bhabba (1992) calls "performative terms"— that is, in terms of the political struggles over social and economic exploitation, political disenfranchisement and cultural and ideological repression. (p. xxi)

So having considered what it isn't, let us define, for these purposes, what it is. The neutral definition of race is category: category of animal or people. These categories are determined by physical traits: skin color, hair color, and facial features. Generally, the human race is divided into three specific categories: Caucasoid, Mongoloid, and Negroid. But there is an aperture between the physical definition and physical experience and the social definition and social experience of race.

The social definition of race was created and is performed. It is continuously created and performed in our lives and in our classrooms as well.

The Bill of Rights for Racially Mixed People, by Maria P. P. Root (2003), states that all biracial people have the right not to justify their existence, not to separate the races within them, not to be responsible for people's discomfort with their physical ambiguity, and not to justify their ethnic legitimacy. Also, biracial people have the right to identify themselves differently than strangers expect them to identify. They have the right to identify differently in different situations, and they have the right to change their identities over a lifetime and more than once. These rights appropriately apply to the experience of being a biracial person, but they can certainly extend to apply to anyone and the ways that race shapes and informs their lives (p. 2).

We should resist the static ways in which race shapes our lives, identities, and pedagogy. This is the first step: resisting and rejecting the impact that racism has on our worlds.

Race as a Social Construction

The practice of sorting human beings based on scientific differences is deeply problematic, and in fact, has no genetic basis. In fact, there is more variation amongst the racial categories than between them. (PBS) The social construction of race, however, has been an effective tool for rationalizing and justifying the enslavement and subjugation of human beings for economic and legal purposes. The US, specifically, is founded on a slavery economy. In order to rationalize the system of slavery and the conflict with the declaration that all men had a right to equality, the social construction of the racial hierarchy justified enslaving Africans. In the context of schools, teacher must learn (or unlearn) the colorblind approach to race they may have been raised with and instead bring this understanding of race to bear on their own work. Amanda Lewis helps us to focus even more by clarifying that "Race is at play all the time inside and outside of schools. It is part of what is happening in our many daily interpersonal interactions. It is one lens through which people read the world around them and make decisions on how to act, react and interact." When we focus our own vision in this manner we are able to see that much more in our students as their worlds (Lewis, p. 300).

Standard

A standard is a benchmark or a unit of measure. There is nothing inherently wrong with standards. They give us guidelines and checklists that help us to determine if our students have mastered certain skills that they will need to move forward on their educational journey. Each child has the right to these skills. The United Nations' Convention on the Rights of the Child (1990) states that each child has the right to a compulsory education and that this education should be directed to "(a) The development of the child's personality, talents and mental and physical abilities to their fullest potential" (article 29C). I find it helpful to conceive of these benchmarks as rights instead of standards because it doesn't set up a punitive relationship between the student and the skill. Standards become problematic when the child is punished for not reaching a benchmark that is out of his or her reach because of his or her own development.

They become increasingly problematic when very broad and general standards that do not account for individual learning differences, curricula, and cultures are used to punish students by retaining them or denying them access to other resources or institutions.

A standardized test is given in a controlled and regulated environment, generally the room the test is given in must meet certain criteria, and the test is timed. These tests are usually multiple choice (which makes grading high volumes of them easier), and so they test predetermined, convergent knowledge. These tests are rooted in the ideals of meritocracy and theoretically should give every child fair access and opportunity based on his or her own effort and ability.

Yet when we recognize that curriculum and learning is a highly individual act for each child that we teach, then we must also recognize that assessment of each child will be equally individual. It is impossible to reach and measure each individual experience with a standardized, convergent test. Again, there is nothing inherently wrong with standardized tests, but they become very dangerous when they are used as a sole measure of what a child is able to do.

According to FairTest: The National Center for Fair and Open Testing (2004), we should consider the following things about standardized tests (paraphrased):

- No test is good enough to serve as the sole or primary basis for important educational decisions.
- Test content is a very poor basis for determining curriculum content, and teaching methods based on the tests themselves are harmful.
- Students from low-income and minority-group backgrounds are more likely to be retained in a lower grade, placed in a lower track, or put in special or remedial education programs when it is not necessary.
- In many districts, raising test scores has become the single most important indicator of school improvement. As a result, teachers and administrators feel enormous pressure to ensure that test scores go up. Schools narrow and change the curriculum to match the test.
- Tests that measure as little and as poorly as multiple-choice tests cannot provide genuine accountability.
- The U.S. is the only economically advanced nation to rely heavily on standardized testing, and yet, because other nations evaluate students on the basis of projects, activities, and essays, without the heavy focus on standardized tests, their students test higher on them. (p. 1)

Many of us are in difficult positions when it comes to standardized testing. We may work in schools or districts like the schools described above. Many communities, parents, students, and teachers have organized to protest the dramatic impact that standardized testing has had on their work and on their lives. It is important to research and, when possible, connect with these groups in order to facilitate change or, even better, understand our own experiences.

Annotated Bibliography

Alliana's Toni Morrison Webpage. Retrieved September 12, 2003 from www.Alliana-Morrison. com

Anderson, L. W., & Krathwohl, D. R. (2001). A taxonomy for learning, teaching, and assessing: A revision of Bloom's taxonomy of educational objectives. New York: Longman.

Appiah, K. A., & Gates Jr., H. L. (Eds.). (1996). *The dictionary of global culture*. Toronto, ON: Vintage.

Apple, M. W. (1990). *Ideology and curriculum*. New York, NY: Routledge.

Apple, M. W. (2001). *Educating the right way*. New York, NY: Routledge. Applied Research Center.

This text is dense and succinct. Outlining the hegemonic, ideological, and systematic nature of power and resources, it draws a very short and straight line between these forces and our classrooms. Have your post-it notes and highlighters ready; you will find that every passage in this book confirms your sense of things and answers your questions. This is one of many books that new teachers must read before they begin their journey.

Michael Apple writes and lectures about power and education. He is one of the most important critical theorists we have. He is a friend to teachers and students. While his work takes on the intense and difficult nature of how power, politics, race and class impact our classrooms, it always manages to be hopeful and empowering.

Apple, M. W. (2007). Retrieved May 26, 2007 from www.arc.org

Asante, M. K. (1991). The Afrocentric idea in education. In W. L. Van DeBurg (Ed.), *Modern black nationalism: From Marcus Garvey to Louis Farrakhan* (pp. 288–94). New York, NY: New York University Press.

This book is a handbook of sorts, and a bible to me. While it does not solely address educational issues, the chapters on education are essential. It also gives a good overview of how some of the best thinkers in American History thought and into how issues of race and politics shape our world and classrooms.

Asim, J. (1990). Black poets for the new millennium. *Black Issues Book Review, 1*, 25–27.

Ayers, W., & Quinn, T. (2005). Series forward. In G. Mitchie (Ed.), *See you when you get there* (pp. vii–ix). New York, NY: Teachers College Press.

Banks, J. A., & McGee Banks, Cherry, A. (Eds.). (1999). *Multicultural education*. New York, NY: John Wiley & Sons.

Bennaly, K. *Accomplices not allies: Abolishing the ally industrial complex 2014*. Retrieved from http://www.indigenousaction.org/accomplices-not-allies-abolishing-the-ally-industrial-complex/

Bencruiscutto, B. (1996, October). *The Populist Movement as seen by L. Frank Baum*. Letter to author.

Berger, K. S. (1994). *The developing person through the life span*. New York, NY: Worth Publishers.
    This is another book that you will borrow from and constantly return to. Anyone who doubts the failure of our schools to build curriculum programs that give all children the right tools and needed information to become contributors in a democratic and socially just world needs to read this book. For those who do the work of fighting for social justice, this book will help to identify the problems with prepackaged, ineffectual programs in our schools while also offering suggestions on how to make authentic, critical programs work instead.

Berry, K. (2004). Radical critical thinking: Part 2: The practice. In J. L. Kincheloe & D. Weil (Eds.), *Critical thinking and learning: An encyclopedia for parents and teachers*. Westport, CT: Greenwood Press.

Beverly, J. (2000). Testimonio, subalternity, and narrative authority. In N. K. Denzin & Y. S. Lincoln (Eds.), *Handbook of qualitative research 9* (pp. 555–566). London & New Delhi: Sage Publications, Inc.

Bloom, B. (1956). *Taxonomy of cognitive domains*. New York, NY: Longmans, Green.

Bohman, J. (2005). Critical theory. In E. N. Zalta (Ed.), *The Stanford encyclopedia of philosophy*, Winter 2003. Retrieved from http://plato.stanford.edu/entries/criticaltheory/

Bornstein, M., & Lamb, M. (Eds.). (1998). *Developmental psychology: An advanced textbook*. Hillsdale, NJ: Lawrence Erlbaum Associates.

Britzman, D. P. (1995). Is there a queer pedagogy? Or, stop reading straight. In W. F. Pinar (Ed.), *Curriculum: Toward new identities* (pp. 211–231). New York, NY: Garland Publishing.

Brown, S., Race, P., & Smith, B. (1996). An assessment manifesto. In 500 tips on assessment. *Kogan Page*. Retrieved February 19, 2004 from http://www.city.londonmet.ac.uk/deliberat ions/assessment/manifest.html

Bruner, J. (1994). The importance of structure. In G. Willis & W. H. Schubert (Eds.), *The American curriculum: A documentary history*. Westport, CT: Praeger Publishers.

Carroll, L. (1897). *Alice in Wonderland: A Norton critical edition* (2nd ed.) (D. J. Gray, Ed.). New York, NY: W. W. Norton Company.

Chennault, R. E. (1998). Giving whiteness a black eye: An interview with Michael Eric Dyson. In J. L. Kincheloe, S. R. Steinberg, N. M. Rodriguez, & R. E. Chennault (Eds.), *White reign: Deploying whiteness in America* (pp. 299–327). New York, NY: St. Martin's Griffin.

Chicago Public Schools. (2005). *CPS at a glance*. Retrieved May 26, 2006 from http://www.cps. k12.il.us/AtAGlance.html

Ciolli, R. (1984). *The politics of textbooks*. Retrieved November 16, 2006 from http://www.alicia patterson.org/APF0701/Ciolli/Ciolli.html

Clarke, J. H. (1994). *The significance of the African world*. In Education for a new reality in the African world. Retrieved November 16. 2006 from http://www.nbufront.org/html/Masters Museums/JHClarke/EdRealityAfricanWord/EdWorldPart10.html

The condition of education: Participation in education. Racial/ethnic distribution of public school students. Retrieved September 8, 2007 from http://nces.ed.gov/programs/coe/list/index.asp

    Clarke spent his entire life researching and documenting the contributions of Africans and those of African descent to the world throughout history. His work completely decenters history as we know it and is crucial reading for any teacher, historian, or otherwise.

Cook, D. (2000). The aesthetics of rap. *Black Issues Book Review*, 2(2), p. 22.

Cooper, B. Retrieved from http://www.alternet.org/news-amp-politics/11-things-white-people-can-do-be-real-anti-racist-allies (p. 1).

Cozzens, L. (1998a). Plessy v. Ferguson. *African American history*. Retrieved May 26, 2006 from http://www.watson.org/~lisa/blackhistory/post-civilwar/plessy.html

Cozzens, L. (1998b). Brown v. Board of Education. *African American history*. Retrieved May 26, 2006 from http://www.watson.org/~lisa/blackhistory/earlycivilrights/brown.html

Cummings, E. E. (1954). *Maggie and Milly and Molly and May*. PoemHunter.com. Retrieved November 2, 2005 from http://www.poemhunter.com/p/m/poem.asp?poet=6588&poem=28828

Davis, B., Sumara, D., & Luce-Kapler, R. (2000). *Engaging minds*. Mahwah, NJ: Lawrence Erlbaum Associates.

    The definition of hypertext and its history as a concept. John Hopkins University Press. Retrieved March 2, 2004 from http://www.cyberartsweb.org/cpace/ht/jhup/history.html#1

Delpit, L. (1995). *Other people's children*. New York, NY: New Press.

    Straightforward and unflinching, Lisa Delpit's work takes a hard look at the educational experience of children of color in schools that are taught predominantly by white teachers. Every teacher should read her books honestly and not be afraid if they sometimes see themselves. Lisa Delpit gives us the how. Using real voices and stories, she shows us the problems and suggests the answers.

DelFattore, J. (1986, Spring). Contemporary censorship pressures and their effect on literature textbooks. *ADE Bulletin*, 83, 35–40. Retrieved June 6, 2006 from http://www.mla.org/ade/bulletin/n083/083035.htm

Denzin, N. K., & Lincoln, Y. S. (Eds.). (2000). *Handbook of qualitative research*. London & New Delhi: Sage Publications, Inc.

Dewey, J. (1959). My pedagogic creed. In M. E. Dworkin (Ed.), *Dewey on education: Selections*. New York, NY: Teachers College Press.

    John Dewey is probably the most read and recognized educational theorist. His focus on development, the role of doing, and child-centered, holistic education has tremendously influenced what we learn about education. Every teacher should do the work to contextualize his theories within the greater realm of critical educational theory.

Dickinson, G. H. *Afrocentric vs. Eurocentric worldviews*. Retrieved November 8, 2005 from http://dickinsg.intrasun.tcnj.edu/diaspora/views.html

Dinges, B. (1990, February). One-third of victims: Black youths are city's top murder risk. *Chicago Reporter*. Retrieved May 26, 2006 from http://www.chicagoreporter.com/1990/02-90/0290%20Onethird%20of%20Victims.htm

DuBois, W. E. B. (1973). *The education of black people*. New York, NY: Monthly Review Press.

Author of the famous book The Souls of Black Folks, and one of the founding members of the NAACP, DuBois is one of the most important writers, thinkers, and activists of our time. While not an outright educational theorist, knowledge and awareness of DuBois and his contributions to our lives are crucial for both teachers and students.

Edgerton, S. H. (1993). Toni Morrison teaching the interminable. In C. McCarthy & W. Crichlow (Eds.), *Race, identity and representation in education* (pp. 220–35). New York, NY: Routledge.

Eggen, P., & Kauchak, D. (1997). *Educational psychology*. Upper Saddle River, NJ: Prentice Hall.

Eurocentric and Afrocentric Worldviews. (2005). Retrieved November 8, 2005 from http://dickinsg.intrasun.tcnj.edu/diaspora/views.html

Evans, M. (1993). Viva Noir! In D. Worley & J. Perry (Eds.), *African American literature: An anthology of nonfiction, fiction, poetry, and drama*. Lincolnwood, IL: National Textbook Co.

Exercise My Rights. Title IX. Retrieved May 26, 2006 from http://www.titleix.info/content.jsp?content_KEY=184&t=higher_ed.dwt

FairTest: The National Center for Fair & Open Testing. *How standardized testing damages education*. Retrieved February 18, 2004 from http://www.fairtest.org/facts/howharm.htm

Foshay, A. W. (2000). *The curriculum: Purpose, substance, practice*. New York, NY: Teachers College Press.

Freire, P. (2000). *Pedagogy of the oppressed*. New York, NY: Continuum.

Gadamer, H. (1996). *The enigma of health*. Stanford, CA: Stanford University Press.

A Brazilian educator who focused on adult literacy, Freire became, arguably, one of the most significant educational theorists ever. Many educators credit Freire with opening their eyes to the political nature of teaching and to their role as agents of change and justice as teachers. Responsible for developing the problem posing method of teaching and for introducing the notion of Conscientization, learning as becoming critically conscious, Paulo Freire is the one writer we cannot do without.

Garcia, H. S., & Valenzuela, T. (2004). Gaining access to critical literacy: Rethinking the role of reading programs. In J. L. Kincheloe & D. Weil (Eds.), *Critical thinking and learning: An encyclopedia for parents and teachers* (pp. 278–280). Westport, CT: Greenwood Press.

Garvey, M. (1920). Declaration of rights of the Negro peoples of the world. In W. L. Van DeBurg (Ed.), *Modern black nationalism: From Marcus Garvey to Louis Farrakhan* (pp. 24–31). New York, NY: New York University Press.

Controversial and inspirational, Marcus Garvey, a Jamaican Nationalist, is most widely recognized for his influence of the Rastafarian Movement and for the Back to Africa movement. Marcus Garvey is another of the great American thinkers and is essential to understanding the roots of African-American culture and history.

Gates, H. L., Jr. (1992). *Loose canons—Notes on the culture wars*. New York, NY: Oxford University Press.

It is generally agreed that Dr. Henry Louis Gates Jr. has done much to bring the college classroom into the American living room. The majority of his work is approachable and meaningful to a wide audience. His work to bring recognition to other African-American writers has helped to broaden the entire terrain of African-American culture. It is because of this that he has been able to turn academic achievement into global celebrity. His presence on the academic landscape alone defeats the stereotypes that African-Americans have long fought against. He has also helped to validate and expand the study of African-American history in our schools and universities. This will have a lasting influence on how the cultural, political, and intellectual contributions of African-Americans in this country will be perceived in academia and throughout the rest of the world. Gates has made a very significant contribution to the literary and research worlds with his large and very exceptional body of work.

Gordon, L. R. (2000). *Existentia Africana*. New York, NY: Routledge.

GLSEN. (2002). *California's legal victory protects teachers*. Retrieved June 1, 2006 from http://www.glsen.org/cgi-bin/iowa/educator/library/record/1174.html

Greene, M. (1988). *The dialectic of freedom*. New York, NY: Teachers College Press.

Greene, M. (1993). The plays and ploys of postmodernism. *Philosophy of Education*. Retrieved October 2, 2001 from www.lesley.edu.journals

Greene, M. (1995). Teaching as possibility: A light in dark times. *Philosophy of Education*. Retrieved October 2, 2001 from www.lesley.edu.journals

    Maxine Greene wants us to stay awake and to realize the importance of the arts and creative expression in our classrooms and in the lives and identity formations of our students. Her books, which include Landscapes of Learning and Releasing the Imagination, are crucial not just for Art teachers, but for all teachers.

Groening, M. (1990). *Lisa's substitute* [Television series episode]. In The Simpsons. Fox Television.

Groening, M. (1996). *Who shot Mr. Burns?* [Television series episode]. In The Simpsons. Fox Television.

Groening, M. (1997). *Bart goes to military school* [Television series episode]. In The Simpsons. Fox Television.

Gubrium, J. F., & Holstein, J. A. (2000). Analyzing interpretive practice. In N. K. Denzin & Y. S. Lincoln (Eds.), *Handbook of qualitative research* (pp. 487–508). London & New Delhi: Sage Publications, Inc.

Hale, J. E. (1982). *Black children: Their culture, roots and learning styles*. Baltimore, MD: John Hopkins Press.

    In my estimation, this is one of the most important books ever written about educating black children. This is a handbook, and, if you are looking for the how and the why, reading this book is critical. Using theory to support her ideas for practice, Hale provides multiple tools to use to be stronger, compassionate educators.

Hare, N. (1969). Questions and answers about black students. In W. L. Van DeBurg (Ed.), *Modern black nationalism: From Marcus Garvey to Louis Farrakhan* (pp. 160–171). New York, NY: New York University Press.

Higgenbotham.

    A lawyer, judge, writer, and professor, A. Leon Higgenbotham brings a unique perspective to the dialogue about race, class and education. His work outlines the legal underpinnings of race in education and is invaluable because it helps us see how the injustices we face in schools today are a result of years of carefully constructed laws and directives. Higgenbotham gives us proof. He also gives us hope. When we understand the construction, we can understand the deconstruction.

Hilliard.

Much of Hilliard's work is concerned with the plethora of contributions that African-Americans and people of African Descent have made to the world as we know it. He is also one of the loudest voices and champions for the new generations of contributors and how their potential should and can be nurtured.

Hirsch, E. D., Jr. (1987). *Cultural literacy: What every American needs to know*. Boston, MA: Houghton Mifflin.

Hogeland, L. M. (1994). Fear of feminism: Why young women get the willies. *Ms. Magazine* (Nov./Dec. 1994). Retrieved November 3, 2005 from http://www.rapereliefshelter.bc.ca/volunteer/fearoffem.html

hooks, b. (1989). *Talking back*. Boston, MA: South End Press.

hooks, b. (1994). *Teaching to transgress*. New York, NY: Routledge.

bell hooks' writing is often in response to her own experience as a member of the educational system and the academy—both as student and teacher. She cites Paulo Freire as a mentor because he was the first theorist she read who spoke of the potential for "learning to be liberatory" (hooks, 1994, p. 7). In much the same way, because she believes in the power that learning has to free our students from their individual situations of poverty and oppression, because she speaks to a particular black, female experience, and because she has carved a path as an educator, fearlessly charting her own journey, doing her own work, and because she is endlessly hopeful about education, love, and the human experience, she is an inspiration to any reader.

I can easily recommend her books to anyone, especially teachers, and I often do. Although she is an established member of the academy, her work is especially useful because her language and her approach are real and accessible. Her perspective and advice do not fly over the heads of the people whom they are meant to reach. Instead they come from her real life experiences, her observations and struggles, and thus they speak to her audience in a way that I believe distinguishes her from every other theorist.

Hudak, G. M. (1993). Technologies of marginality: Strategies of stardom and displacement in adolescent life. In C. McCarthy & W. Crichlow (Eds.), *Race, identity and representation in education* (pp. 174–187). New York, NY: Routledge.

Jencks, C., & Phillips, M. (Eds.). (1998). *The black-white test score gap*. Washington, DC: Brookings Institution Press.

Kanpol, B. (1998). *Critical pedagogy for beginning teachers: The movement from despair to hope*. Retrieved March 18, 2008 from http://users.monash.edu.au

Karenga, M. (1998). From The Nguzo Saba (The Seven Principles): Their meaning and message. In W. L. Van DeBurg (Ed.), *Modern black nationalism: From Marcus Garvey to Louis Farrakhan* (pp. 276–287). New York, NY: New York University Press.

Kilebard, H. M. (1999). *Schooled to work: Vocationalism and the American curriculum, 1876–1946*. New York, NY: Teacher's College Press.

Kincheloe, J. L. (1991). *Teachers as researchers: Qualitative inquiry as a path to empowerment.* New York, NY: Falmer Press.

Kincheloe, J. L., & McLaren, P. (2000). Rethinking critical theory and qualitative research. In N. K. Denzin & Y. S. Lincoln (Eds.), *Handbook of qualitative research.* London: Sage Publications.

Kincheloe, J. L., & Steinberg, S. R. (1997). *Changing multiculturalism.* Philadelphia, PA: Open University Press.

Kincheloe, J. L., Steinberg, S. R., & Gresson, A. D., III. (Eds.). (1996). *Measured lies: The Bell Curve examined.* Toronto, ON: OISE.

Kincheloe, J. L., & Weil, D. (Eds.). (2004). *Critical thinking and learning: An encyclopedia for parents and teachers.* Westport, CT: Greenwood Press.

Kozol, J. (1992). *Savage inequalities.* New York, NY: Harper.

Kubrick, S. (1999). *Eyes wide shut: A screenplay.* New York, NY: Warner Books.

Kunjufu, J. (1990). *Countering the conspiracy to destroy black boys* (Vol. 3). Chicago, IL: African American Images.

> The work of Jawanza Kunjufu focuses primarily on young African-American men, but it is applicable to every classroom. This eye-opening series gives us both how and why. Like the work of Janice Hale, Kunjufu's work helps us to be aware and compassionate educators.

Ladson-Billings, G. (2000). Teaching in dangerous times. *Re-thinking Schools, 14*(4).242–250.

Lewis, A. E. (2003). Everyday race-making: Navigating racial boundaries in schools. *American Behavioral Scientist, 47*(3), 283–305.

Lindsey, R. B., Robins, N., & Terrell, R. D. (1999). *Cultural proficiency: A manual for school leaders.* Thousand Oaks, CA: Corwin Press.

Luthi, M. (1976). *Once upon a time: On the nature of fairy tales.* Bloomington, IN: Indiana University Press.

MARGARET Fund of the National Women's Law Center. (2005). Title IX facts & myths. *Title IX, I exercise my rights.* Retrieved May 26, 2006 from http://www.titleix.info/content. jsp?content_KEY=179

May, W. T. (1993). In S. D. LaPierre & E. Zimmerman (Eds.), *Research methods and methodologies for art education.* Reston, VA: National Art Education Association.

McCarthy, C., & Crichlow, W. (Eds.). (1993). *Race, identity and representation in education.* New York, NY: Routledge.

McIntosh, P. (1998). *White privilege: Unpacking the invisible knapsack.* Retrieved November 8, 2003 from http://www.utoronto.ca/acc/events/peggy1.htm

McKenzie, M. (2015). *8 ways not to be an "ally": A non-comprehensive list.* Retrieved from https://www.bgdblog.org/2013/06/20136178-ways-not-to-be-an-ally/

Michie, G. (2005). *See you when we get there: Teaching for change in urban schools.* New York, NY: Teachers College Press.

Milner, H. R. (2010). A diversity and opportunity gaps explanatory framework. In Start where you are, but don't stay there: Understanding diversity, opportunity gaps, and teaching in today's classrooms (pp. 13–44). Cambridge: Harvard University Press.

Morrison, T. (1970). *The bluest eye*. New York, NY: Penguin Books.

Toni Morrison is one of the mostly widely read and admired American authors of the late 20th century. Beginning her career as an instructor and editor, she went on to become a renowned force in the world of literature. Having written fiction, plays, political essays, children's literature, and opera, her creativity has few limits. Her reach and influence has extended from politics to film to rap music. Known for turning the enigmatic history of the African-American people into compelling and haunting stories, her writing has shaped and inspired people's lives.

With her novels, Morrison has established a place for herself among the classic authors whom she admired and honored with her earlier work. She has already left a very visible footprint on American culture. Her political writing is also far reaching and influential. While she first worked to shape and to nurture the work of others as a teacher and editor, she has become a muse to other important artists. The rap artist and actor Mos Def was inspired to write a song with Talib Kweli for their first album together entitled "Thieves in the Night." This song borrows a passage from The Bluest Eye and, like The Bluest Eye, examines the impact of racism on American culture.

Morrison is also one of the most widely decorated and esteemed writers of this century. In addition to her Pulitzer Prize, she is one of nine women, and the only African-American woman, to be awarded the Nobel Prize for Literature. She continues her work as a writer, cultural critic, and as professor at Princeton University as the Robert F. Goheen Professor in the Council of Humanities. Among the many distinctions she holds, she is also the first black woman to be appointed a Chair at an Ivy League University.

National Organization for Women (NOW). (2005). *Talking about affirmative action*. Retrieved November 2, 2005 from http://www.now.org/issues/affirm/talking.html

Neihart, M. *The social and emotional development of gifted children: What do we know?* PowerPoint presentation by Carol Ann Thomas.

Nicholson, D. R. (1998). Developing a media literacy of whiteness in advertising. In J. L. Kincheloe, S. R. Steinberg, N. M. Rodriguez, & R. E. Chennault (Eds.), *White reign: Deploying whiteness in America* (pp. 193–212). New York, NY: St. Martin's Griffin.

Office of the High Commissioner for Human Rights. (1990). *Convention on the rights of the child*. Geneva: Office of the United Nations High Commissioner for Human Rights. Retrieved February 18, 2004 from http://www.unhchr.ch/html.menu3/b/k2crc.htm

One Nation/One California. (1997). *English for the children*. Retrieved June 6, 2006 from http://www.onenation.org

PBS. (2004a). *Time and place: Slavery and the making of America*. Retrieved May 26, 2006 from http://www.pbs.org/wnet/slavery/timeline/1739.html

PBS. (2004b). *Time and place: Slavery and the making of America*. Retrieved May 26, 2006 from http://www.pbs.org/wnet/slavery/timeline/1817.html

Perry, T., & Delpit, L. (Eds.). (1998). *The real Ebonics debate: Power, language, and the education of African-American children*. Boston, MA: Beacon Press.

Pinar, W. F., Reynolds, W. M., Slattery, P., & Taubman, P. M. (Eds.). (2000). *Understanding curriculum*. New York, NY: Peter Lang Publishing.

For those who want to tread into the deeper waters of curriculum theorizing, the writing of William F. Pinar will challenge you and make you smarter. His writing will wake you up. You may find yourself asking how any of this relates to what you are dealing with in your classrooms on a daily basis, but after spending some time with his work, you will come to see that we cannot afford not to question our work at this level. Even though it is hard work, you will not regret it.

Powell, J. (1997). *Derrida for beginners.* London: Writers and Readers.

Reinharz, S. (1992). *Feminist methods in social research.* New York, NY: Oxford University Press.

Richardson, L. (2000). Writing: A method of inquiry. In N. K. Denzin & Y. S. Lincoln (Eds.), *Handbook of qualitative research* (pp. 923–948). London & New Delhi: Sage Publications, Inc.

Roderick, M. (2006). Closing the aspirations-attainment gap: Implications for high school reform, a commentary from Chicago. *MDRC.* Retrieved November 14, 2006 from http://www.studentclearinghouse.org/highschools/pdfs/MDRC_CPSstudy.pdf

Root, M. P. P. *Bill of rights for racially mixed people.* Retrieved December 16, 2003 from http://www.mixedfolks.com/rights.htm

Rossman, G. B., & Rallis, S. F. (1998). *Learning in the field: An introduction to qualitative research.* Thousand Oaks, CA: Sage Publications.

Sautter, R. C. (1994). *Who are today's city kids? Beyond the "deficit model."* Retrieved May 18, 2006 from http://www.ncrel.org/sdrs/cityschl/city1_1a.htm

Schwab, J. J., Westbury, I., & Wilkof, N. J. (1978). Science, curriculum, and liberal education: Selected essays. Chicago: University of Chicago Press.

Shaw, R. P. (2000). *The educational theory of Maxine Greene.* Retrieved October 2, 2001 from www.lesley.edu.journals

Slattery, P. (1995). *Curriculum development in the postmodern era.* New York, NY: Garland Publishing.

Sleeter, C. E., & Grant, C. A. (1999). *Making choices for multicultural education.* Hoboken, NJ: John Wiley & Sons, Inc.

Smith, D. G. (1996). Identity, self and other in the conduct of pedagogical action: An east/west inquiry. In W. F. Priar (Ed.), *Contemporary curriculum discourses: Twenty years of JCT* (pp. 458–473). New York, NY: Peter Lang Publishing.

St. Classis, R. (2003). *Learning the science of pedagogy.* 21st Century Science and Technology Magazine. Washington, DC: 21st Century. Retrieved February 19, 2004 from http://www.21stcenturysciencetech.com/articles/Summer03/learning.html

Stankiewicz, M. (1997). Historical research methods in art education. In S. LaPierre & E. Zinnermann (Eds.), *Research methods for art education* (pp. 55–73). Reston, VA: National Art Education Association.

Stephenson, W. D. (2002). *Homeland security requires Internet-based thinking—Not just technology.* Retrieved November 8, 2005 from http://www.homelandsecurity.org/journal/Articles/Stephenson0102.htm

Stone, L. (Ed.). (1994). *The educational feminism reader.* New York, NY: Routledge.

Stovall, D. (2005). *Communities struggle to make small serve all.* Rethinking Schools Online, 19, 4. Retrieved June 1, 2006 from http://www.rethinkingschools.org/archive/19_04/stru194.shtml

Strinati, D. (2004) An introduction to theories of popular culture (2nd ed). New York, NY: Routledge.

Tatum, A. W. (2005). *Teaching reading to black adolescent males: Closing the achievement gap.* Portland, ME: Stenhouse Publishers.

Thomas B. Fordham Institute. The mad, mad world of textbook adoption. Retrieved June 6, 2006 from www.edexcellence.com

Tozer, Steven., Senese, Guy., & Violas, Paul. (2015). School and Society: Historical and Contemporary Perspectives. McGraw-Hill College.

Van DeBurg, W. L. (Ed.). (1997). *Modern black nationalism: From Marcus Garvey to Louis Farrakhan.* New York, NY: New York University Press.

Villaverde, L. E. (2004). Developing a curriculum and critical pedagogy. In J. L. Kincheloe & D. Weil (Eds.), *Critical thinking and learning: An encyclopedia for parents and teachers* (pp. 131–134). Westport, CT: Greenwood Press.

Wallace, I., & Wallechinsky, D. (1978). *The people's almanac.* New York, NY: Bantam.

Waltonen, K., & Du Vernay, D. (2010). The Simpsons in the Classroom: Embiggening the Learning Experience with the Wisdom of Springfield. Jefferson, NC: McFarland.

Waters, H. F. (1990, April). Family feuds. *Newsweek, 23,* 58–64.

Watkins, W. H. (1993). Black curriculum orientation: A preliminary inquiry. *Harvard Educational Review, 63,* 321–337.

Watkins, W. H. (2000). *The white architects of black education: Ideology and power in America, 1865–1954.* New York, NY: Teachers College Press.

This article was crucial to my development as a young teacher and I would recommend this to anyone starting out on a journey as an educator. If you are interested in the history of the construction of racism, especially within the institution of education, William H. Watkins is the expert.

West, C. (1999). *The Cornell West reader.* New York, NY: Basic Civitas Books.

A self-described "non-Marxist socialist" and "Radical Democrat of African Descent," Cornell West is one of the giant scholars of race, class, economics, culture, gender and social justice today. His work examines everything from classical literature to pop culture to art and music theory to parenting. He is master of both the emotional and intellectual domains. Any time you spend with the work of Cornell West is going to leave you smarter and with a better understanding of your role as an educator and cultural worker.

White House, The. *President Bush signs landmark education reforms into law.* Retrieved November 14, 2006 from http://www.whitehouse.gov/infocus/education/

Wikipedia. *Affirmative action.* Retrieved May 26, 2006 from http://en.wikipedia.org/wiki/Affirmative_action

Wikipedia. *Demographics of Chicago.* Retrieved June 6, 2006 from http://en.wikipedia.org/wiki/Demographics_of_Chicago

Wikipedia. *Ghetto.* Retrieved November 3, 2005 from http://en.wikipedia.org/wiki/Ghetto

Wikipedia. *Institutional racism*. Retrieved May 22, 2006 from http://en.wikipedia.org/wiki/Insti tutional_racism

Wikipedia. *Literacy test*. Retrieved May 26, 2006 from http://en.wikipedia.org/wiki/Literacy_test

Wikipedia. *Slave codes*. Retrieved June 6, 2006 from http://en.wikipedia.org/wiki/Slave_codes

Woodson, C. G. (2000). *The mis-education of the Negro*. Chicago, IL: African American.

    A scholar and historian, Woodson was interested in researching and documenting the lives of prominent and every day African-Americans. He is the originator of the annual celebration we know today as Black History Month.

Woodson, C. G. (1998). *The education of the Negro*. New York, NY: A & B Publishers.

Worley, D. A., & Perry, J., Jr. (Eds.). (1994). *African American literature*. Lincolnwood, IL: National Textbook Co.

Studies in Criticality

General Editor
Shirley R. Steinberg

Counterpoints publishes the most compelling and imaginative books being written in education today. Grounded on the theoretical advances in criticalism, feminism, and postmodernism in the last two decades of the twentieth century, Counterpoints engages the meaning of these innovations in various forms of educational expression. Committed to the proposition that theoretical literature should be accessible to a variety of audiences, the series insists that its authors avoid esoteric and jargonistic languages that transform educational scholarship into an elite discourse for the initiated. Scholarly work matters only to the degree it affects consciousness and practice at multiple sites. Counterpoints' editorial policy is based on these principles and the ability of scholars to break new ground, to open new conversations, to go where educators have never gone before.

For additional information about this series or for the submission of manuscripts, please contact:

Shirley R. Steinberg
c/o Peter Lang Publishing, Inc.
29 Broadway, 18th floor
New York, New York 10006

To order other books in this series, please contact our Customer Service Department:

(800) 770-LANG (within the U.S.)
(212) 647-7706 (outside the U.S.)
(212) 647-7707 FAX

Or browse online by series:
www.peterlang.com